a.

MAD DOG

MAD DOG

JOHNNY ADAIR

with Graham McKendry

JOHN BLAKE

Published by John Blake Publishing Ltd,
3 Bramber Court, 2 Bramber Road,
London W14 9PB, England

www.blake.co.uk

First published in hardback in 2007

ISBN 978 1 84454 339 7

British Library Cataloguing-in-Publication Data:

A catalogue record for this book is available from the British Library.

Design by www.envydesign.co.uk

Printed and bound in Great Britain by William Clowes Ltd,
Beccles, Suffolk

1 3 5 7 9 10 8 6 4 2

Papers used by John Blake Publishing are natural, recyclable products made
from wood grown in sustainable forests. The manufacturing processes
conform to the environmental regulations of the country of origin.

Every attempt has been made to contact the relevant copyright-holders, but
some were unobtainable. We would be grateful if the appropriate people
could contact us.

FOREWORD

When asked by a journalist in the mid-1990s if he had ever had a Catholic in his car, Johnny Adair replied 'only dead ones'. This was the first time I had ever heard of the man.

While shocking, this throwaway comment seemed to fit the image that most outsiders held (and still hold) of the Loyalist paramilitary – vicious, nakedly sectarian, and, as one commentator argued, having all the 'political nous of a rottweiler'. In fact, so typical and expected was this caricature for many, that little serious attention has ever been paid to the remarkable story of Northern Ireland's once most powerful paramilitary movement, the Ulster Defence Association, or UDA, and those within it.

The UDA's main objective was to uphold Northern Ireland's place within the United Kingdom. Until the eventual proscription of the pro-State movement by the British Government in 1992, the UDA remained a legal organisation using a series of cover names, such as the Ulster Freedom Fighters and Ulster Defence Force.

Because of the UDA's eventual descent into criminal activity, collusion with the rogue members of the security services in Northern Ireland and other various sinister events, it is easy to dismiss the UDA as never having had genuine political aspirations. Consequently, for years Loyalism, in all its forms, has gone largely unexamined, and this is why its significance continues to remain poorly understood.

In fact, it seems unbelievable even now that the UDA was once a formidable power that could command extensive social and political influence, yet in the early 1970s, the then 40,000-strong movement brought Northern Ireland to a virtual standstill by organising a general strike through the Ulster Workers' Council (led by several senior UDA members). The UDA's objective had been to bring about several reformist measures in Ulster, notably the abolition of the Northern Ireland Executive and greater political representation at Westminster.

Yet, one decade later, and following the assassination in 1987 of arguably its most effective and strategic leader, John McMichael, the UDA's decline was set firmly in motion. By 1989, the movement was in complete disarray, and the security services in Northern Ireland had finally succeeded in virtually paralysing the movement.

Ironically, it was a major journalistic investigation by Roger Cook into the movement's racketeering and extortion activities that combined with other events to ultimately lead to the UDA's internal reshuffle. There was a change of leadership and revitalisation with younger, fresh recruits who would each play their part in the UDA's new attempts to rearm itself from local, national and international sources. With the UDA energised, the movement returned as a dangerous force in the early 1990s, with Loyalist terror groups surpassing even the Provisional IRA in assassinations, murders and casualties.

In 1994, less than two months after the Provisional IRA declared its 'complete cessation of military operations', the UDA and sister movement the Ulster Volunteer Force (UVF) called their own ceasefires. For the first time the residents of Northern Ireland were given the hope of peace whilst the contending sides of the conflict engaged in dialogue rather than fighting with each other and the British government.

While much of the commentary surrounding the ceasefire period at the time might be characterized as both naïve and premature, there were some overlooked developments within Loyalism that remain poorly understood.

The Loyalist position was that much of the political change in Northern Ireland seemed to have been at their expense (at least until the recent surprising resurgence of Ian Paisley's DUP). Loyalist marginalisation had been a deliberate policy of the then leading Nationalist movement, the Social, Democratic and Labour Party (SDLP) that sought to go directly to the Irish or British government motivated by a concern to limit and perhaps abolish the historical 'Unionist veto'.

However, for the first time in many years, political initiatives after the ceasefire offered (and even guaranteed) the Loyalist community a voice in the political process and the future shape of Northern Ireland. That the Loyalist paramilitaries enthusiastically participated and remained in this process despite the collapse of the PIRA ceasefire is worthy to note. And while the process would go on to expose the rivalries between the paramilitary and constitutional Loyalist political parties, by at least recognising the voice of Unionism, the ceasefire discussions guaranteed an outcome of compromise rather than a complete victory.

Of course, in the days immediately after the ceasefire, celebrations in Northern Ireland did not suggest a popular recognition of any impending compromise (indeed, 17 months later, the ceasefire would break down amid acrimonious accusations of bad faith and other issues). But on 1 September, 1994, celebrations in Republican areas had a distinctly triumphalist quality and there was a popular sense that the ceasefire represented a step towards the establishment of a united Ireland.

As the process developed, however, so too did it become clear that Unionism, far from being marginalised was being brought to centre stage. Juxtaposed against this development, the ruling Conservative Party's weaknesses forced a greater dependence on the Unionist vote in Parliament, further strengthening the Unionist's bargaining position.

Just over one year into the ceasefire, the collapse of which would be heralded by a massive Provisional IRA bomb in

London, former Northern Ireland Secretary of State Mo Mowlam took the unprecedented (and risky) step of acknowledging the critical role of the prisoners in supporting the peace initiative when she visited the notorious Maze Prison in Belfast. Among those she met was Johnny 'Mad Dog' Adair.

Jailed in 1995 for membership of the UDA's Ulster Freedom Fighters and for directing terrorism, Adair was nothing less than an icon. Feared, hated and reviled in some quarters, idolised and revered in others, Adair remains both an enigmatic and divisive figure. His story makes for reading that is as uncomfortable and unsettling as it is breathtaking in its audacity set against a chaotic backdrop of some of the worst atrocities of the Northern Irish troubles.

Several dozen Catholics were murdered, often in horrendous circumstances, by the unit that Adair commanded. C Company, and indeed the UDA overall, never successfully shook off the image of being blatantly sectarian. The stunning discovery that members of the security services fed intelligence to the UDA only demonised it as typical of Northern Ireland's 'dirty war'. Convinced by Mowlam of the merits of supporting political representatives, Adair was released four years into a 16-year sentence.

Ironically, the 1994 ceasefire also served as the catalyst for years of savage internecine feuding which ripped apart the remains of the once formidable Loyalist groups. Despite positive early signs, the UDA's representatives failed to establish an effective political presence in the wake of the ceasefire. The UDA, in Adair's words, imploded. With no IRA to fight, the movement would turn inward, unclear of its purpose and place within a rapidly changing political scene in Northern Ireland.

Since 2000 the UDA has degenerated into movement torn apart by territorial jealousies, competition over the proceeds of organised crime and continued differences over political aspirations and loyalties. Jealousies, bitter rivalries and a series of personality clashes have conspired to see the UDA kick Adair out of the organisation in 2002 for his efforts to link the UDA with the Loyalist Volunteer Force (LVF). Some viewed Adair's work as an attempt to consolidate his power and influence over the combined Loyalist command.

With Adair in and out of prison during this time, the UDA began its housekeeping in earnest and the remnants of once mighty C Company were systematically dismantled. Adair and his family would eventually take temporary refuge, first in England, then Scotland. Since then, all who have pledged allegiance to him have been left alienated and at risk.

This book presents the remarkable account of a man once at the heart of Loyalist terrorism. It is a brutal, graphic, sometimes absurd and frequently unsettling autobiography. Adair has survived over a dozen assassination attempts on his life, many of which caused as much destruction as his would-be assassins claimed to be preventing by killing Adair.

FOREWORD

In some ways, what is presented here is an attempt to understand this man and the events in which he participated. It goes without saying that this is a risky and contentious business. Former RUC Chief Constable Sir Ronnie Flanagan once remarked that 'understanding' paramilitaries in Northern Ireland came 'dangerously close to authorising, sanctioning and approving.'[1]

He is correct in this, but although understanding may indeed come with an uncomfortable price, it is a cost worth bearing in order to learn how someone like Johnny Adair became wrapped up in the chaos of the Troubles and went on to lead the most feared Active Service Unit in all of militant Loyalism.

It is a case from which there is much to be learned and it is only the beginning of a series of accounts from Northern Ireland that may yet take much time to emerge. Some never will.

In fact, it is remarkable that Johnny Adair is even alive to tell his tale. Despite significant leaps forward in the peace process since those eventful days of the UDA's virtual disintegration, it offers him little security. Despite the fact that Adair says he sleeps soundly at night, he will forever be looking over his shoulder. A spray painted wall in Belfast once warned that he, and long-time mentor John White, were 'dead men walking'.

He now lives far from Northern Ireland, and from the heartland once ruled by he and C Company. He ominously

1 T Harnden and G Jones, 'Early release of terrorists under attack', *Daily Telegraph*, 4 February, 1999.

pledges to return. As what, and how, only time will tell, but while this book tells the story of his eventful life so far, its final chapter will almost certainly not be Adair's last.

John Horgan
Senior Research Fellow Centre for the Study of Terrorism and Political Violence University of St Andrews

PREFACE

Many will find it unpalatable that I have written my autobiography.

There will be concerns I am exploiting the horrors of the Troubles for my own profit. I am also sure that no matter what reasons I give to justify this book there will be those who think there are disingenous and will remain unsatisfied.

But the fact is, there have been countless versions and accounts of my life put into the public arena with no input from myself and it is time for me to tell my story.

This is a straight account of my life growing up on the streets of Belfast and making my way to the top of the UDA. Despite being forced from my home and being betrayed by people I would have died for, I have not sought to settle scores in these pages.

I am genuine when I say I wish my story didn't need to be told. I certainly didn't want to grow up in the middle of a war zone, spend so many years hiding from snipers bullets and be seperated from my family behind bars. But I did.

I grew up in Protestant Belfast and that is what we believed in and fought for. We laid everything on the line to protect our community from Republican attack. This book is an account of how I first became involved and the battles that we fought. I do not wish to glorify violence or seek to exploit any of those who lost their lives. In these pages you will learn what happened to me and those around me.

Those days are over now and if the conflict in Northern Ireland has taught us one thing it is that violence solved nothing. This is a historical document and I hope it helps to move the peace process forward by drawing a line under what happened. My war is long since over and I hope that a full and proper peace will come to Northern Ireland.

JA

ACKNOWLEDGEMENTS

I would like to thank my very best friend, who for over thirty years has been loyal and true to me – Samuel 'Skelly' McCrory. Thanks for everything. There are many other friends and supporters who have stood by me. However, for reasons of security they must remain anonymous. You know who you are.

I would like to take the opportunity to salute the bravery and the dedication of all the men and women who I once commanded. You remained true to the cause in defending Ulster from attack for almost thirty years.

While most of the UDA leadership sat back in the comfort of their luxury homes and got rich, you put everything on the line for what you believed in. It saddens me that many have been left to rot by the current leadership. I think about you all every day and wish that I could be there. But, as the motto says 'Quis Separabit', we will never be separated in thought and indeed in person. Watch this space.

Jock Lamb, Ian Truesdale, Woodsy, Willie, Wildcat, Big Hughie, Stephen, Vo, Wee Puffy, David Malone, Donal Mac, Mickey Carrol and all the boys from Norfolk. All the boys from Salford. The cute boy and all the shit bags from Bolton. Colin Bell, Snowball, Andy, Wee Jimmy, the Glasgow crew.

Also thanks to my friends who are currently serving time in HMP Maghaberry, HMP Bowhouse, HMP Magilligan, HM YOC Hydebank.

My friend in Mid Ulster, you know who you are.

A very special thanks to the men and women from north, south, east, west and south east Antrim UDA Brigades who continue to keep in touch with me. Big respect to you all. Ulster Resistance, Press Eye.

Big thanks also to Mad Nick, Christiane, Chris, Anna, Mikey and all my friends in Dresden, Germany. All the boys in the Real McCoy (keep my bed warm), Double Top (Kilmarnock), Jean Houston, Andy and Janice. All the Christian men and women who have been very supportive to me and my family in recent years. God bless you all. Natalia (Portadown). I would also like to thank my wee hero, aka super Prod.

And to the photographers Kelvin Boyes and Brian Anderson.

Last but not least my family. A massive thanks to my mother, brother and my sisters. I love you and miss you dearly.

ACKNOWLEDGEMENTS

Gina, Natalie, Chloe, Jonathan and wee Jay love you all from the bottom of my heart.

A special thanks to Graham McKendry who over the months showed patience and dedication while helping me with the book. Cheers bud.

Johnny Adair

My involvement in this book would not have been possible without the help and support of numerous people. First I would like to thank my colleagues at the Scottish *News of the World*. In particular Brian Anderson for his work behind the lens and Gary Jamieson on the picture desk. Thanks. Also to David Leslie and Craig Jackson for all the encouragement.

Thanks also to everyone at John Blake for making it possible to work on the project and ensuring it was as painless as possible. And to Johnny himself for asking me to help with the book.

Finally, a very special thanks to my friends and family who put up with me during the summer of 2006. In particular to my mum, dad, sister and SW for correcting my spelling and being there. Love you all.

Graham McKendry

CONTENTS

Introduction		xxi
1	The Buzz	1
2	Knocked Back	17
3	Old Guard, Young Turks	27
4	Loss and Gain	37
5	Heroes and Traitors	47
6	New Blood	61
7	Eyes and Ears	79
8	Settling Scores	91
9	Betrayal	105
10	Face to Face	123
11	Aborted	139
12	The Crum	151

13 A Better Class of Prison   165

14 Back Inside   189

15 An Ancient Feud   207

16 Exiles   221

17 The Peace Dividend   239

Key Characters   251

Glossary   255

INTRODUCTION

I didn't see the gunman coming. It was over an hour into the gig when he made his move. The only light illuminating the faces in the crowd came from the stage. My features were slightly disguised by a beanie hat pulled down on my head, but he knew it was me.

I heard the bang of the gun a split second before I felt the pain. It was excruciating. Pulling my hand back from Gina, my wife, I clamped it to the side of my head. I knew what was happening. I was sure I didn't have long left.

Gina spun round to see what was going on. I could see her lips moving but there was no sound. I wasn't going to collapse to the ground and no way would I scream and shout. If these were my last seconds, I was going to be strong.

As the people around me struggled to work out what was going on, I felt my hat being removed; it was saturated with blood. Everything was happening in slow motion. I turned round to eyeball the gunman but he was gone.

With my hat off, people realised who I was. It was clear I wasn't going to get any help. One guy hurled a pint of beer in my face while the others kicked me to the ground. They weren't part of the murder bid but they couldn't believe their luck. Johnny 'Mad Dog' Adair, maimed with a bullet in the head right in front of them: time for some revenge.

I could see even less lying on the ground surrounded by the furious mob. Shafts of light came and went as kick after kick shook me. Gina and a friend were trying their best to hold my attackers back. I was hemmed in by a security barrier, but as the blows rained down I managed to prise it apart. I stumbled into an open patch and got a moment's respite. But the mob poured through the gap after me and tried to inflict more damage. Twice more I was taken down but I managed to get back on my feet and broke free again. I staggered away, occasionally stopping, turning and trying to fend them off, before moving away as far as I could and then repeating the manoeuvre.

All the while I could hear Gina screaming for help. Nobody wanted to know. I managed to grab her and we headed for the protection of a security man in a fluorescent jacket. My face was covered in blood, so at first he didn't recognise me and I hoped there was a chance he might get me out of there. But the IRA were running security that night and he turned his back and walked away. Gina and I were on our own now.

As fast as we could, we made our way out through the

exit and on to the road. I clocked a taxi sitting at a give-way waiting for the traffic to clear. Frantically, I shuffled over, opened the door and jumped in. The cabbie knew who I was and did what he was told. The crowd threw some rocks at the car but we were in the clear. The driver, who I later learned was a Catholic, asked if I wanted to go to the hospital. That wasn't an option. If it was the IRA who had been behind the hit, they would find out where I was and finish off the job. It was back to my house off the Shankill Road.

I'd believed I was no longer seriously at risk. It was April 1999 and Northern Ireland was in the middle of the peace process. Sure, there would always be a Nationalist who would have killed me, given the chance, but they weren't competing with one another for the honour, as they had done in the early 1990s.

Even so, when the security team arrived to pick me up from the Maze Prison the day before the concert, some measures had to be taken. Around 15 men kitted out with radios and earpieces kept an eye on what was going on as I walked through the gate and got into one of the cars.

Coming out of prison was always a bit dodgy, as gunmen would have a good idea where you were going to be and when. But afterwards I would have the protection of the Loyalist community where I lived.

Once the UDA's C Company security team were ready, we sped off back towards my home. In more dangerous days, it was common for a switch to be done en route so that any spotters waiting outside the prison would pass on incorrect details to any ASU planning an ambush. But I was happy that no change-over was needed now and I was convinced there was no risk in going to the gig. I couldn't believe my luck when Gina told me that UB40 were playing in Belfast on a day when I was out on pre-release parole. I'd always been a big fan and I thought we would have a great night out.

By contrast, my minders weren't at all happy about me going to the concert. Even though I wasn't going into the heart of Republican Belfast, they were convinced there was a chance of trouble and wanted to send a team along with me. I wasn't having any of it. Being surrounded by minders and heavies was only going to attract more attention. The guys had bought me a new Vauxhall Vectra, so Gina and I travelled in it to Belfast's Botanic Gardens and planned to drive back. That way I was out in the open for less time.

That evening, the sun was still shining and I could hear the PA system as we got closer to the venue. As we made our way through the security check, I spotted a few faces I knew, all friendly, so there was nothing to worry about. Gina and I stood at the back of the venue, ready to enjoy the gig.

When the first band came on, a couple in the crowd started to look out of place. A tall guy and a woman had walked past us a couple of times, clearly checking me out. At first I hadn't noticed them, but Gina was suspicious. Then they made their move. They strode towards me, the guy in front and the woman right behind him. I took a couple of steps forward to take any fight away from Gina. As I got closer to the man, he shouted out my name and

XXIV

nodded. I was relieved. It turned out I'd met him on a previous parole day. He was a friend of someone who knew my family and had come round to the house to have his picture taken with me. It was the only time during the whole evening that I was suspicious of anyone.

After the attack, the taxi driver took us to the home of trusted UDA man William 'Winkie' Dodds. My face was swollen from the beating and I was covered in bruises, but I could live with the pain. The C Company security team were brought together and it was decided I should be taken to the Ulster Hospital on the outskirts of the city. There were three other hospitals the IRA would check before that one if they were looking for me, and now I had the team with me to watch my back.

When I got to the hospital, I was expecting to be briefly looked at and taken straight through to surgery. As it happened, the hospital had very little experience in dealing with gunshot wounds. The nurses looked at me bemused as I explained that I'd been shot in the head, that there was only one hole and this meant the bullet was still lodged in my skull. They weren't convinced. When I told them the round must have been damp, which would have prevented it from doing proper damage, it confused things even more and I got the impression they didn't believe me. Eventually, I was taken for an X-ray and the slug showed up. Only then did they realise there was a problem.

'Mr Adair, we have discovered a round in your head,' the doctor told me. Well, I knew that. 'The good news is it's safe. You can have a bed for the night here or you can go home and come back in the morning, when there'll be a surgeon here'.

It was a night of freedom from my cell in the Maze, and the last thing I wanted to do was spend it on a hospital ward. It was a tough night. I didn't get home until the early hours and then, every time I put my head down, the pounding pain came back, so I hardly slept at all. My thoughts were veering from who was behind the attack to how lucky I'd been.

In the morning, I was re-examined, this time by a specialist, who told me that I would have to have the bullet taken out at some point but there was no hurry. I didn't see the point in hanging on. If it was going to have to be done, it might as well be then and there.

In the theatre, I was given a local anaesthetic and so I was awake throughout the procedure. Although I couldn't feel any pain, I could hear the medical instrument scraping my skull as the surgeon tried to get the bullet out. At one point, the medical team had to stop and give me another painkilling injection because the slug was deeper than they thought.

I saw the bullet when it was removed and dropped into a shiny silver dish. It was huge, a big lump of lead, and I was shocked. I knew my stuff and I'd guessed I'd been shot with a .22 round. This was way bigger than that. The doctor put it into a test tube and it was taken down to the police and we all had a look at it. Our best guess was that it was from a .38 and had been lying around getting damp since the Second World War.

INTRODUCTION

When I got back to the Maze, I was sent for by the governor, who told me that he couldn't believe the call when it came through from the hospital. A nurse had telephoned to say I was going to be late returning as I'd been shot in the head, but not to worry: I would be back. The governor didn't know whether it was a wind-up or not.

The next concern was the backlash. The peace process being brokered by the British and Irish governments was at a delicate stage and the last thing the security services wanted was a witch-hunt. There were a number of reprisals without my knowledge but I called a halt to them as soon as I could. I met our spokesman, John White, and said, 'I am alive, I have been through this before, and I don't want the peace process wrecked.'

Word came through from the Republicans that the attack was nothing to do with them and I believed them. It was the best opportunity anyone ever had to kill me. He was firing from point-blank range and if it had been the Provisional IRA they wouldn't have made a mess of it. Alternatively, they could have left a bomb under my car and blown me to bits.

The police were panicking and weren't convinced that I wouldn't let it escalate. The last thing they wanted was bodies turning up all over the city while the talks were going on. Two senior detectives came to question me in the Maze and let me know they had no evidence to suggest it was Republicans behind the hit. They were anxious to see what I was thinking about it, but I had no idea and told them so.

After showing me my beanie hat with the bullet hole in it, they asked me, 'OK, what about Eddie? Do you know Eddie?'

My first thought was Eddie Copeland, a leading Republican activist in north Belfast, but again they insisted it was nothing to do with him. They were certain it was Catholic hoods who had seen an opportunity to kill me and given it a go. Did they have a weapon on them at the gig? Or did they spot me and send out and get one? I was there for hours, so they would have had the chance. Whoever it was had the nerve to get close to me and hold the gun in the middle of a packed concert. He knew what he was up to. Only one round was fired, but the guy knew that from close range this was all that was required. To have fired more would have given him less time to flee the scene.

The IRA murdered one of the main suspects. Ed McCoy was a 28-year-old drug dealer from the south of the city who was killed by IRA men masquerading as Direct Action Against Drugs. In May 2000, he was drinking in the pub with friends when two gunmen wearing false beards walked up behind him and shot him in the head and body. The gunmen's getaway car was later found abandoned. McCoy was given a massive blood transfusion but died the next day. Other drug dealers that he had links to were also killed by the IRA.

The other name I was given came from a Catholic prisoner in Maghaberry. He came into my cell one day and threw down a newspaper that contained a memorial notice for someone called Whiteside. He was probably the guy who had shot me, and now he had committed suicide. His name meant little to me. I was just glad to be alive.

1

THE BUZZ

Violence was a way of life on the Shankill Road. Growing up there as a kid was like having the biggest and best playground right on your doorstep. There was always danger, always something happening, and that was what made it so exciting. I was born on Sunday, 27 October 1963, during a period when Northern Ireland was experiencing relative peace and stability. An IRA border campaign the previous year had disintegrated without getting very much support.

I was the seventh child of Mabel and Jimmy Adair. Our house off the Old Lodge Road in Belfast was right on the front line of the divided Protestant and Catholic communities, slap bang in the middle of what would descend into a war zone. West Belfast would remain my home until my family and I were forced to leave in 2003.

Like any other family in the area, we were poor. My parents, five sisters and one brother and me were all crammed into a traditional two-up, two-down terraced house with an outside toilet. Dad worked at the Ulster Timber Company on Duncrue Street in Belfast Docks, and did his best to feed his family and provide for us all. He was a very quiet man who didn't drink or smoke, and there wasn't a bitter bone in his body.

My family had no history of involvement with paramilitaries and there was certainly nothing there that hinted at the path I would later take. I firmly believe that if I had grown up anywhere but west Belfast I wouldn't have got drawn into the Troubles and spent so many years behind bars, let alone become the leader of the UDA. Growing up on the Shankill wasn't a normal childhood, but it was all I knew. There was no stage when I thought to myself, I want out of this place. Besides, we were a poor family, so where were we going to go? It was what I was born into and what I had to accept.

When I was very young, there was little of the vicious divide and hate-fuelled violence that would rip the area apart. The two communities lived side by side and I clearly remember playing with Catholic kids in the street when I was growing up. They lived alongside us and, as far I was aware, there was no difference between us.

All that changed during a week of violence in August 1969. Tensions had been bubbling under in Northern Ireland for most of the year. Leading Loyalists were unhappy with the liberal attitudes of the Prime Minister,

Captain Terence O'Neill. They believed that his policies were far too moderate, and they were going to do something about it. Forces within the Ulster Protestant Volunteers and the Ulster Volunteer Force collaborated to stage a series of bombings that were made to look like the work of the IRA.

In March of that same year, the Castlereagh electricity substation, which supplied power to the south and east parts of Belfast, had been blown up. The following month, water pipes in Dunadry in County Antrim, the Silent Valley reservoir in the Mourne Mountains and at Lough Neagh were all targeted. The city was brought to its knees and the IRA were getting the blame. O'Neill resigned, but it didn't stop the trouble. Catholics and Protestants in Northern Ireland were now on a collision course.

Trouble first erupted in Londonderry, where Harold Wilson's Labour government had given the go-ahead for the annual Apprentice Boys' march around the city walls on Tuesday, 12 August 1969. The march sparked two days of violence in the Catholic Bogside area of the city and, as word quickly spread, clashes flared up in Belfast.

The people on the Shankill began to feel they were under siege and that the IRA were coming to force them out of their homes. After seeing the trouble in Londonderry, the Irish Prime Minister, Jack Lynch, inflamed the situation in a television address by saying that action was needed and that a united Ireland was back on the cards. Within days, the two communities turned on each other. Rioting and looting left seven people dead. Protestants now knew they were

3

under attack, and a backlash followed that led to Catholics being burned out of their homes.

Only five at the time, I understood very little about what was going on. I remember waking up and finding the street jammed full of police cars and fire engines as they attempted to deal with the mayhem from the night before. While I'd been asleep, a mob had gone to the homes of suspected Catholics and set them on fire. The kids I'd played football with were gone and their homes were still smouldering.

My age didn't prevent me from knowing the difference between a Protestant and a Catholic. I knew also that it was the Catholics who had been forced out of their homes before they were torched. What I didn't know was why.

I remember hearing people say, 'The Taigs have been burned out,' and I'm pretty sure that was the first time that I thought Catholics must be bad people. After that week of violence, everything changed for everyone, and soon it became the norm for us to hate them and them to hate us without question.

As I grew up, the differences between Protestants and Catholics became more extreme and increasingly violent. Our house was only a few hundred yards from the staunchly Republican Ardoyne area, on the front line, where the tension was worst and the conflict most ferocious.

Most nights, from my bed in the attic of the house, I could hear gun battles raging between the British troops and the IRA. My brother Archie and I would listen to the crack of automatic fire and try to work out what was going on. It was frightening and exciting at the same time. I would look out of the window and see the troops, crouching behind protective barriers, open fire, then take cover as their targets returned the attack. This wasn't watching a film or playing with Action Man: it was right on your doorstep and better than any movie you were ever going to see.

When the gun battles really kicked off anyone who was outside was hauled back into the house. All the lights would be turned out and all the family would huddle together in the same room. The scream of the sirens and violent explosions meant that you did what you were told. There was always a risk that a stray bullet might get you, or that armed men might come crashing through the front door. It was so bad that we had to creep about hunched down to get from room to room. Despite the danger – which was the same for every family – you never wanted to miss out on any of the action. Whenever possible, someone would be stationed at the window and give us a running commentary.

The morning after a big battle was always something to look forward to. At first light, I would get up and scour the streets for trophies. Thousands of spent cartridges would be strewn everywhere, and the makeshift shelters that the combatants had used would be peppered with bullet holes. My pals and I would inspect the scarred stone and wonder how anyone had managed to make it through the night.

After a night's trouble, we would also look for bullet

heads that weren't damaged, stick them in a glass of Coke to shine them up and put a hook on them so we could wear them on a chain.

The soldiers were on the streets all the time and any chance I got I would pester them. Most of the time they were happy to show you their guns, take out the magazine full of bullets and let you have a look. They were armed with SLRs loaded with huge brass 7.62mm bullets.

As well as the army, the Tartan Gangs would be roaming the streets. They were shaven-headed teenage Loyalists who hung around on street corners wearing Wrangler jackets and stonewashed jeans with tartan patches, Ulster badges or pictures of King Billy sewn on to them to make sure everyone knew what they were about. They weren't paramilitaries, just teenagers out looking for a fight with Catholic lads. I would watch them getting ready for a fight, or winding up the opposition and think to myself, I want a bit of that action.

I was so in awe of the gangs that I would do everything I could to look the same. They were happy to get us involved at the age of ten, or sometimes even younger. At first, we did simple things, like tipping them off when a car would be coming out of a Catholic area so they could ambush it. There was no thought about who was driving the car; it had come out of a Catholic area so it was good enough to be targeted. They would lie in wait until the word was given the motor was on its way, then they would spring from their boltholes into action, peppering it with stones, bottles, anything they could get their hands on.

THE BUZZ

From there you graduated to the next level: making a petrol bomb. They taught us to get our hands on a large milk bottle, a small amount of petrol, a bit of sugar and a rag, and away we went. Whatever they wanted, sourcing missiles to be thrown or dragging petrol bombs down to the barriers, I was glad to do it. There were thousands of kids on both sides of the peace line who were delighted to get their hands dirty. It was a real buzz and we were proud to be helping the paramilitaries. Many boys want to be soldiers when they grow up. I wanted to be like the uniformed paramilitaries who roamed the streets to protect our community.

It was a war zone, a constant war zone. Almost every night the Tartan Gangs would gather at the top of our street, ready to cause mayhem. All I wanted to do was get stuck in. I was only a kid, but the feeling of running with hundreds of men spoiling for a fight was something else.

When the police or the army turned up to try to keep the sides apart we would just give them a hard time for as long as we could get away with it. Nothing beat getting close to an army vehicle, waiting until the last moment and then throwing your stone inside it as hard as you could. Hundreds of stones would be raining down on the vehicle, but, if you thought one was yours, it made your night.

It was also good to keep in with the UDA guys. As well as looking after the community, they also policed it. I remember wanting to help a guy called Kenny Slavin when I saw him tied to a lamppost. His fingers had been broken, his hands were secured behind his back and he was plastered in blue gloss paint. I used to hang about with his brother and I was about to help him but the UDA men who were standing near by growled at me that he was a housebreaker and sent me on my way.

One of the UDA guys I looked up to was Norman McGrath. I knew him because he lived on Cunningsby Street, round the corner from our house, and I would see him every now and then when I was hanging about on street corners with my friends. Norman was a teenager and the kind of bloke I respected as a role model. He was one of the guys who manned the barricades and defended us against whatever the other side were doing.

In 1971, Norman was gunned down in the street by Republicans who opened fire on him from a passing car. If he had been shot dead I doubt I would have remembered him: he would have been mentioned in passing as the latest man killed. But Norman survived, though he had to have his leg amputated. Before long he was back on the streets, and to me this made him a hero. The IRA had tried to kill him but failed. Norman, the guy who gave me a few pennies to go to the shops with, had taken a bullet for me.

On 11 June the following year, still only 18, Norman was shot dead by British soldiers on Manor Street. There was always trouble at this notorious flashpoint which had Protestants at one end and Catholics at the other. The night Norman was shot, one of the fiercest gun battles took place in Oldpark. At the time locals said he wasn't armed when two soldiers from the Royal Regiment of Wales opened fire on him from close range. But the RUC claimed to have found seven 7.62mm bullet cases close to his body. Experts also told an inquest they couldn't rule out that Norman had fired a gun during the rioting, because of the amount of residue on his cuffs.

What happened to Norman made no difference to our attitude. Nor did the shooting of a pal as we rioted as kids. I was hanging about on Manor Street one evening with my best friend Billy Rea, waiting for trouble to start. The two sides were locked in a face-off, waiting to see who would make the first move. There was the usual trading of insults and missiles. Then, out of nowhere, a gunman appeared. I remember him clearly because he wasn't wearing a hood or making any effort to disguise who he was. He opened fire with a bolt-action rifle. Seeing the weapon and then hearing the bang as he let off a round scared us. Suddenly it was more than just throwing missiles. There was real danger and it was right in front of us.

We dashed for the safety of our end of the street. I was running for my life, with Billy in front of me. The next thing I knew he fell to the ground, almost in slow motion. He had been hit in the foot. My mate was screaming at me, 'I've been shot! I've been shot!' That was the danger of getting involved, but I still loved it. For me, the constant threat of serious consequences was far outweighed by the thrill of being out on the street seeing some action.

It was around that time that a feeling of bitterness started to grow in me. Seeing my community attacked and people getting killed made sure it kept eating away at me. There wasn't a lot my parents could do to stop me getting involved, not least because it was right on your doorstep. It wasn't as if I was getting on a bus and travelling miles to get involved in trouble. It was just there, all the time.

Everyone was in the same boat and the community stuck together. After a night's trouble, the mothers would meet in the street and gossip about what had been going on as they swept up the bottles and rocks that littered the ground.

Whenever I got caught rioting by the police, they would bring me home rather than lock me up. My father cuffed me as much as any other dad, especially when I was getting escorted home by the coppers most nights of the week. But, even though I was the one causing the trouble, he was always sure to have a go at them first. He would give them a mouthful and ask if they had nothing better to do with themselves. I never got away with it, though, because once he was done with them I was next in line.

My father wasn't at all interested in the Troubles. Most of his friends were Catholics, many of them members of the same pigeon club as him. I remember being taken to their homes and told that they were Catholics but they were OK and there was no need to be afraid of them. All the same, the thought was still in the back of my mind that we were on enemy territory.

My father felt that since he had no involvement or interest in any of the fighting he was immune from it. He thought, I'm not a bigot, so I can go where I want and do what I want. It didn't always work like that. He was beaten up while walking his dog in the Waterworks Park because he was a Protestant in the wrong place at the wrong time. It was nothing too serious, just a couple of black eyes and some bruises. Had it not been him, it would have been someone else.

I was in no way a special case, or a kid who had strayed way over the line. There were plenty of other kids in Belfast who were up to exactly the same things.

With all this going on, it is easy to see why I was never really that interested in school. I started in 1969 at Hemsworth Primary School, just around the corner from my house. By the time I started at Somerdale School six years later, I couldn't wait to get out of the system. The only thing that kept my attention was the fighting. On the bus that we took to school there would be Catholic girls going to Our Lady of Mercy School. There were fights nearly every morning. Spitting, kicking, anything went. At nine in the morning on the way to school, and then again at midday when you got lunch from the chippie, you would be fighting with the guys from St Gabriel's. I was always getting brought into school by the police because I spent most of my lunchtimes fighting with Catholic kids from that school. It was petty stuff, but the cops would still lift me and take me back to face my headmaster. I still have scars from the constant fighting.

There were days when we couldn't make it to school because the road had been sealed off after the fighting of the previous night. At other times we would be allowed to pass by burned-out cars, buses and other smouldering wreckage from the skirmishes that had raged just hours before. All the way to the school gates the consequences of the fighting were there in full view.

Most mornings I would get some sweets from the local shop to take to school. But it wasn't always that easy. One day I couldn't get into the shop because the body of a Catholic man had been dumped in the alley next to it. He had been repeatedly stabbed. The police were all over the place trying to stop people getting in the way of the forensic team, but I was still able to see the body lying on the ground, wrapped in plastic sheeting.

The older I got the more I wanted to know what the fighting was about and why our street looked like a war zone nearly every day. When you heard the family talking around the kitchen table about another Protestant man being murdered or wounded for no reason, that was when the hatred started to grow inside you and you wanted to know why it was happening. In fact, in Belfast it was easy to educate yourself. The gable ends of buildings were covered in huge murals that celebrated the heroes of the conflict and there were Orange Walk parades, which were all about displaying our culture. The city was stark in its contrasts, so becoming well versed in your side's beliefs wasn't difficult.

It was also a smart idea to make sure you were streetwise. If you didn't, it was easy to get into all sorts of trouble. There were parts of the city that were no-go zones. Even on your own patch, there was absolutely no guarantee that you were safe.

I was only 13 when I saw the aftermath of the murder of 45-year-old bus driver Harry Bradshaw during the Loyalist workers' strike in May 1977. I was messing about on the roof of the entrance to a derelict cinema on Crumlin Road when the noise of gunfire filled the air as the double-decker bus pulled up. I had the perfect view of everything. After hearing the crack, crack, crack of his weapon, I saw the assassin run up the street with a snorkel jacket done up tight to hide his face. I didn't think twice about getting down off the roof to see what had happened. In situations like this, you had to get there as fast as you could, because the minute the cops turned up they told you where to go.

I remember looking at the driver, still seated at the wheel of the bus, and watching him turn grey in the daylight. One of the passengers had opened his shirt and was trying to help him. I could see the bullet hole, but there was no blood coming out of it. Thinking that this meant he would be OK, I legged it before the police turned up.

A coalition of the UDA and the Reverend Ian Paisley's Democratic Unionist Party had organised the workers' strike. It was designed to put pressure on the politicians who were running the country at the time, but, when it failed to get the community's backing, intimidation tactics were rolled out.

Days before his murder, Harry Bradshaw had been attacked by a female passenger who hit him over the head with an umbrella and insisted that he should take part in the strike. The father of five decided to work instead and as a result was killed.

Kenny McClinton carried out the hit and also that on a Catholic man called Daniel Carville. McClinton was a founding member of the UFF's C Company, of which I would later become military commander. He was one of the hardest men in Ulster, and even when they locked him up he was still fighting with Republicans. Then one day he found God, turned his back on all the violence and became a pastor. He knew my father, and I met him for the first time at my dad's funeral. Throughout most of my time behind bars, he wrote to me telling me to take the route that he had. McClinton had hung around in the same places as I had and thought that for this reason I would respect him and listen to him.

Even as a kid I had the habit of being in the wrong place at the right time. Our main place for hanging about was outside the Royal Antediluvian Order of Buffaloes in Century Street. Known as the 'Buff Club', this was a favourite haunt of prison officers from the notorious Crumlin Road jail, which housed terrorists such as Lenny Murphy, who was one of the 'Shankill Butchers', and the IRA informer Sean O'Callaghan. Outside the Buff Club I would meet up with friends of that time like Jackie Thompson and Mark Rosborough. Sometimes William 'Winkie' Dodds would turn up and join in the drinking on the street.

One night a screw came out of the club, clearly having had a lot to drink. We started to take the piss out of him because he could hardly stand up straight. The next thing, he pulled out a gun and started firing at us. He didn't miss by much. The police were called and later he was thrown out of the Prison Service.

THE BUZZ

When I was 15, I saw the dead body of George Foster at the same place just after he had been gunned down by the IRA. It was 14 September 1979 and I was with a couple of the lads at the usual spot when there was a loud crack of gunfire followed quickly by a screech of brakes. The first thing we did was rush round to see what had happened. I'm not sure what I thought I was going to do when I got there. Foster, who was married with two kids, and three other prison officers regularly went for lunch in the Buff Club and they were returning to work when the IRA gunmen made their move.

Earlier that day, the killers had hijacked the car that was to be used in the hit. Later, around the corner from the club, they sat in the orange Fiat Strada waiting for their targets. When the three men appeared, the IRA team followed them into Century Street and let them get into a car before opening fire wildly. Foster was struck in the head, while one of the other men was hit in both arms. When I got to the scene Foster was already dead, his body slumped in the car. Lying next to the dented car was his blood-spattered pack of Craven A cigarettes. He must have had them in his hand when the assassins struck. Another guy nicked the smokes and puffed away on them. Stealing from the dead – not even I would do that.

Foster, who was 30, had joined the Prison Service two years earlier, having previously been a member of the UDR, an infantry regiment of the British Army. A guy from west Belfast was later given 20 years after pleading guilty to his manslaughter. The gunman also got two life sentences for

15

the killing of two soldiers, Private Christopher Shanley and Lance Corporal Stephen Rumble.

Five days later, just 200 yards away from where Foster was killed, the assistant governor of Crumlin Road Prison, Edward Jones, was shot by the IRA as he sat in his car at traffic lights. A car drew up alongside the father of ten and the gunman unloaded several shots from a large-calibre revolver. Sixty-year-old Jones had worked in the prison for 33 years when they took him out.

Growing up among the rioting and the mayhem that gripped the area was exhilarating for a kid. Of course it was frightening – the flashing lights, the explosions, the tension and hatred – but that was what gave you the buzz. The older I became and the longer I lived in the streets of Belfast, the more the bitterness got a grip of me. I didn't wake up one morning and decide: I want to be a paramilitary. I went through a lot before I got there. The only difference between me and an IRA man is that it says 'Roman Catholic' on his birth certificate and 'Protestant Presbyterian' on mine. But that wasn't going to stop the mutual hatred.

2

KNOCKED BACK

I was never going to stay the course. My constant fighting with Catholic lads meant that I was always in trouble at school, and in the end I pushed it too far and was thrown out in my last year.

Fighting every day with Catholics was what I did and I told myself that by doing it I was helping our community. I was naive to think it would make any difference, but I was desperate to do something useful.

In an effort to get me on the right track, my dad sent me to Crumlin Road Opportunities. This project was part of a scheme introduced across Belfast to tackle the sectarian problem by bringing Protestant and Catholic youths together and teaching them a trade. The guy who ran it was Davey Payne, an ex-UDA leader from the north of the city and a real hard guy. He had been in at the start of the scheme and the government wanted people like him to front workshops in the hope that youngsters like me might respect them and take on board what they had to say. In theory, it was a great idea, but not even Payne was able to stay away from the paramilitaries in the long run.

In January 1988, he was caught helping to transport a massive cache of weapons that had been brought in from Lebanon. Payne was in the lead scout car, followed by two Ford Granadas packed full of weapons, including 61 AK-47 assault rifles, 30 Browning pistols and 150 grenades. He ended up getting 19 years.

For a year I mixed and worked alongside Catholics at the project. Before going to Crumlin Road the nearest I'd got to Catholics was fighting with them in the street. Now I was being forced to work alongside them. For six weeks you learned a new trade, for instance joinery or upholstery, and they hoped that you would then go on and use it in the real world and settle down. The money was rubbish, though; my first pay packet was just £19.50.

When the weather was bad, the rain would pour in through gaps in the roof, but I couldn't really complain too much about that. Years earlier I'd been taken to court after being nabbed stealing lead off the roof to take it to a scrap dealer and make a few quid.

At first I felt bitter about just being made to be in the same room as Catholics. They were the enemy and were making our lives a misery, so why should I be put in this situation? The theory was that once we got into the workshop everything else was to be left at the door. It could have been a chance for things to go in a different direction for me. I spoke with the Catholics and realised that on their side of the peace line it was very tough, almost a mirror image of our side. But it always came back to the same thing: fighting and rioting. I went through the motions, while at the back of my mind there was always suspicion of the Catholics alongside me.

It was the early 1980s and tensions in Northern Ireland were at their very worst. The IRA hunger strikers were trying to get better conditions granted to them while behind bars and violence was erupting on the streets every night.

The skinhead revival had also kicked off in a big way and I was right in among it. It suited me to join up, as the skinheads were real tough nuts, much more than the mods. By this stage, every Saturday night without fail I and the rest of the gang would get loaded up on cider and take a bus into town to look for trouble. You had to be properly prepared, so before leaving the house I would get my best jeans on, polish up my boots and shave my head.

A lot of the time the fighting would be with the Catholics who were on placement at Crumlin Road Opportunities. If they were voting for Sinn Fein or giving them any sort of support, they were killing Protestants, so that meant they were fair game.

As well as the music and the clothes, for a lot of us the skinhead thing included signing up for the National Front. In Belfast at that time there were no black people or other foreigners, so being in the NF wasn't about race hatred but about being British and the fact that it gave us another way of targeting the IRA.

For three years it was a big deal to me. Sam 'Skelly' McCrory, Brian Watson, Julian Carson and I formed a band called Offensive Weapon. I played – well, tried to play – a bass guitar for which I'd paid a massive £200. I was rubbish and could manage only two chords. When we started playing gigs, Brian would have to keep me right and make sure that I was doing something vaguely like I was supposed to be.

For us a lot of it was about the excitement of renting big amps in town, handing out tickets and putting up posters. Then hundreds of people would turn up and we would play six or seven songs. It didn't matter that we were dreadful; the crowd loved it. We wrote about what was going on in Northern Ireland at the time, songs like 'Gestapo RUC', 'Smash the IRA' and 'Bulldog'.

It was through the skinhead scene that I met Gina Crossan, who later became my wife. I was at a party and spotted her, with her head shaven apart from a small bleached blonde tuft at the front. She was from Shankill Parade, not far from where I lived. Before long we became very close, as were very well matched. On 23 August 1984, we had our first child, Jonathan, born at Belfast's City Hospital. We gave him the middle name Paul, after Gina's brother, and Samuel after my mate Skelly. I was 21 when Jonathan came along, which might seem young to some people, but it wasn't that big a deal, as there were plenty of couples in the same situation.

We got a small flat on Shankill Parade, upstairs from Gina's mother, and did it up. It was a very happy time and we would go out drinking with her mother every Saturday night to all parts of the city and have a laugh. Like everyone, we had our ups and downs, but Gina was always my rock.

At this time I was still hanging about with the boys from the band and we would travel out to places like Bangor in County Down, to get away from the city. On one of the trips I lost the top of one of my fingers. I was full of cider, really hammered, and we were getting on the train to go back home when someone slammed the door of the carriage shut on my hand. It was agony. Sam picked up the severed bit of finger – about a centimetre long – and put it in his pocket, hoping that when we got to the hospital doctors might be able to save it. There was nothing I could do until we got back to Belfast except try to deal with the pain. A member of staff had phoned ahead so that when the train pulled into the station the police were there to take me to hospital, but by the time we arrived at A&E it was too late to save my fingertip.

As a result of the accident I got £1,900 compensation, and Gina and I felt we were the richest people in the world. It was the most money either of us had ever had and we set about enjoying it. Although I worked, I'd never earned enough to go away on holiday before. For our first holiday together we had a brilliant two weeks in Blackpool and returned home with our bags packed full of new clothes.

The fact that I was now a dad didn't stop me from going to National Front meetings. These had to be held in secret, as the RUC would have stepped in if they had known what was going on. So Sam and I would meet up at a pub and wait to be told where the meeting was about to be held, to prevent details of the venue being leaked.

In September 1983, I helped organise a National Front march from Belfast City Hall to the Shankill. But the real home of the NF was London, so I travelled there a couple of times to attend meetings, go to gigs and buy the latest skinhead fashions. The Last Resort on Petticoat Lane, in the East End, was the shop to go to, and you weren't a real skinhead until you bought your gear from there.

London was also the place to see the best skinhead bands, like Skrewdriver. In November 1983, after seeing a gig, Skelly and I got caught up in some heavy fighting. The result was an assault charge and an appearance at Camberwell Magistrates' Court, where I was ordered to pay £100 compensation.

I went over to London on the bus a couple of times to see Skrewdriver play, and on one trip there were some Catholic skinheads from the Falls Road. All the way there they were begging me and Sam not to tell the English skinhead crew we were going to see where they were from, as they were petrified they would get a real going-over.

The first time I went there I couldn't believe London. It was so different from Belfast and I'd never seen anything like it before. The skinhead thing at the time was to share a squat, and I would have loved to do that. Skelly and I even got to meet the lead singer of Skrewdriver, Ian Stuart. I was infatuated with the whole movement, and here I was sitting in a cafe with the singer of the band I loved and he was buying us toast and tea. I couldn't believe it was happening. But the problem was that I had a job and I couldn't just jack it in and disappear to London.

My parents weren't happy that I was involved with the skinheads. Every weekend they knew I was going out fighting, and they had no idea what injuries I would come back with. Between my first conviction in July 1981 and my appearance at Camberwell in 1983, I was done 16 times, for disorderly behaviour, criminal damage and assault, but none of my court appearances had resulted in prison. I just picked up a fine every time.

At the time I was only ten stone, but I was game and had no fears about getting stuck into whatever was put up in front of me. I regularly woke up in hospital with new wounds, and that would get me more grief from my mother about the fighting. To this day I'm covered in scars from being smashed over the head with bottles or police batons.

When I was 18, my parents decided there was no talking to me, and they were probably right. Instead of going to the youth club and playing snooker, we preferred to get some cider and head for the city centre, on the lookout for a fight.

By the time I'd reached the top of the UDA and was serving time for my involvement, I tried to keep my parents from knowing more than they needed to. The fact that I'd ended up in prison was nothing to do with them at all. During all the time I was locked up, I think I sent them only one access pass to visit me. As far as I was concerned, the Maze wasn't the sort of place that my dad would want to be seen. It was my fault I was behind bars, and there was no way I was going to bring more shame on him by making him come there.

My father and I were completely different. For years he worked away at the timber yard and did his best for the whole family. Once I'd completed the course at Crumlin Road Opportunities, he made sure that I got the first vacancy that came up at the yard.

Both Protestants and Catholics were working there and I clearly remember my first day at the job. By this stage I'd built up a bit of a reputation for fighting, but of course that wasn't the case with my dad. He could walk through Catholic areas like the New Lodge without any trouble. We walked together to the timber yard, but for me it wasn't the most comfortable way to get to work, because if I'd been spotted I would have been dragged up an alley and got in all sorts of trouble.

It got worse when we reached the yard. There was an RUC reservist who worked alongside my dad, and the first thing I heard when I arrived that first day was one of the other workers saying to him, 'I think I know his face,' to which the copper replied, 'I know his face – from the back of a police Land Rover.' Thankfully, it was a joke, but my card was marked.

The trouble I'd been getting into backfired on me when I tried to sign up for the Ulster Defence Regiment. I wanted to do more than be a street fighter, as I was sure I had other skills to offer. My plan was to sign up for the UDR on a part-time basis and do something legitimate to fight our corner. By giving a couple of nights a week to the regiment, I thought, I'd be doing my bit to take on the IRA.

To start with, I went to night classes at the UDR centre on Malone Road, where they assessed if you were the sort of person they wanted in the regiment. If I made it through the selection process, I would then act as a back-up for the regular forces and the RUC. The prospect excited me and I was determined to make the grade. I knew that my convictions would be a problem, but a guy who was already in the UDR took me aside and told me he had made it through selection despite having a few marks against his name. That really got my hopes up. I would be doing something on the right side of the law, protecting the community

It didn't happen. Instead I got a letter saying that I had been rejected. I'm sure that Special Branch had a hand in it. They would have known who I was and that I was fighting all the time, and warned the UDR that I was trouble. What made the knock-back all the harder to take was the fact that I'd been given a bit of hope that my convictions wouldn't count against me. I'd convinced myself that I would make it despite my record. Now there was only one option left if I was going to take the fight to the Republicans.

3

OLD GUARD, YOUNG TURKS

It wasn't long before I started getting noticed by the UDA leadership. The Shankill is a pretty small place and it was no secret that there was a hard core of us who were regularly fighting with Catholics. They saw me as someone who was bitter and game to get his hands dirty. That was just what they wanted.

The problem at the time was that the UDA was a shambles run by drunks who were little more than small-time bullyboys. The last thing they were was a military organisation who were able, or even willing, to take on the Republicans. Virtually no operations were being carried out and the commanders were more interested in making sure that they had enough money to cover their drinks bill in whichever of the 86 pubs on the Shankill that they used.

If they weren't boozing, they were in the bookmaker's placing bets, or coercing kids into petty crimes to fund the rest of their day. My father, on his way home from work, would walk past them as they lay slumped in doorways. He used to say they were nothing more than 'scumbags who never worked or wanted'.

None of us had any interest in signing up to become part of that. If I was going to volunteer, it would be to join the UVF, as at the time they were the only ones taking the fight to the Nationalists. But in the end I didn't have a choice. One night I was summoned off the streets to the UDA headquarters and told that I had to sign up.

The guys in charge stank of booze and barked at us that they knew everything we were up to. The first time they asked us to join I managed to dodge it. But within days I was hauled back in and it was made clear that unless I did what I was told I would be taking a bullet.

Donald Hodgen, Jackie Thompson and Skelly were all in the same boat. None of us wanted to get involved with the UDA but we were all made an offer we couldn't refuse. While the UDA guys were drunks, they would still have had no problem shooting you if you didn't do what you were told. The four of us were told that we had to be back at the headquarters in a week for the swearing-in ceremony, otherwise there would be trouble.

In reality, what was supposed to be an initiation into a paramilitary organisation was little more than a shambles that confirmed what we all thought about the UDA. There were no hoods or guns, just two men holding a bit of paper.

One by one we were made to read out the oath and soon it was my turn:

> I, Johnny Adair, am a Protestant by birth and, being convinced of a fiendish plot by republican paramilitaries to destroy my heritage, do swear to defend my comrades and my country, by any and all means, against the Provisional IRA, INLA, and any other offshoot of republicanism which may be of similar intent. I further swear that I will never divulge any information about my comrades to anyone and I am fully aware that the penalty for such an act of treason is death. I willingly take this oath on the Holy Bible witnessed by my peers.

It was all a load of nonsense and I saw nothing in the early days that convinced me otherwise. The only reason they wanted new faces was to bring them more of the £1 weekly dues that had to be handed over by each member. But there was no way to get out of it. The last thing they were going to let you get away with was not turning up with the money. If you let them down, they wouldn't think twice about coming round to your house, dragging you into the street and battering you senseless in front of your wife and kids.

I still desperately wanted to see action and take on the IRA, who were slaughtering our people. But the UDA in their present state weren't going to allow me to do that. Skelly, Hodgen, Thompson and I were all placed in the C8 brigade. The only way I could see us breaking free of the mess was to get into the Ulster Freedom Fighters, the UDA's military wing. But the UFF hadn't been seen or heard of in years. The rest of the organisation was rotten and choked with intelligence informants, so with no alternative on the horizon I just got on with being an ordinary member, paid my dues and kept my head down.

I remember one of the senior members walked into a room half-cut and assembled a sawn-off shotgun. He put two cartridges in before turning round, pointing the weapon at us and slurring, 'I'm looking at all youse now. If anybody ever thinks of escaping, or gives a statement when arrested, I'll blast you to death myself.' That was the extent of their military ability.

The first time I was called on to carry out any sort of operation was when I was told to help hijack a bus. The UDA were fighting for segregation for Loyalist prisoners, who were mixed in with Republicans in Crumlin Road jail. We were sent out to hijack a bus to help create the pressure they wanted to put on the authorities. A number of operations had been planned for that night, but ours was the most elaborate. Everything went according to plan and we caused a bit of grief.

A couple of weeks later, one of the guys from the hijacking team was lifted by the police for something unconnected. He cracked and, in exchange for dropping the other charges he was facing, offered them details of who had been involved in grabbing the bus. Within hours the police broke down my father's front door, arrested me and took me to the Castlereagh Holding Centre under the Prevention of Terrorism Act of 1974.

It was the first time I was lifted under the Act and I felt proud. But at the same time I'd heard the stories about the infamous Castlereagh. Suspected terrorists from both sides were taken there and interrogated. If the authorities didn't get what they wanted that way, it was beaten out of you.

I managed to get through the first interview. I was asked if I was a member of any paramilitary organisation. I denied it. They put it to me that I'd hijacked the bus. Again I denied it. I was beginning to feel I had nothing to worry about, as they were giving me everything they had yet they had nothing on me.

Then the pressure was turned up. The detective leading the questioning was a tall thin guy with swarthy skin. Just before the first session ended, he said to me, 'Now listen, you. I'm going to lock you up now, and when I come back I'm going to show you the proof that you hijacked the bus, and when I do that you're going to be in trouble.'

I was still convinced they had nothing, so by the time he came back in to have another go I was feeling pretty cocky. I'd made it through the first interview and I hadn't been battered or nailed to the table. Clearly the stories I'd heard were wrong, or I was too smart for them.

Then the copper came back into the room. He was pretty casual, peeling an orange and drinking milk from a carton. Then he threw a bit of paper down on the table and asked me to read it. It was a blow-by-blow account of what had happened, signed by the guy who had cracked. It was authentic and I knew I was in trouble. I had no idea what to do. The UDA hadn't given us any schooling on what to do if you were arrested under the Prevention of Terrorism Act. I thought the statement meant that I was done and there was no way out of it. I decided to try to bluff my way out of it. I told the detective that his source must be lying. For that I got a cuff across the side of the head, then another. It was the first time I'd been put under any sort of pressure, and I coughed to the lot.

The result was that I was remanded until my court date. Although I had 'previous', it was all minor offences, and when I appeared I was handed a suspended sentence.

While I was on remand, one of the guys went to see the commander of C8 to get my welfare money, which is paid out to prisoners while inside. All he was told was that he would see what he could do. It would have been just £7 a week, but it was drinking money that they were losing out on. To make matters worse, the rat who had stuck me to save his own skin was left alone. I was promised that retribution would be handed out, but nothing happened. All it did was make me realise more and more that the UDA was decaying at the core. All I could do was hope that somewhere down the line the UFF would make a reappearance and offer me an out. During the 1970s they had been the main players in carrying out anti-IRA operations. A resurgence of the UFF would let me get away from the deadwood, who were just in it for the free booze.

Things improved when I was asked to try out for the elite Ulster Defence Force. It had been set up in 1983 and was the brainchild of the UDA's number two, John McMichael. The idea was to take the youngest and keenest volunteers and see what they were made of, while at the same time training them up in combat techniques. A camp was set up at Magilligan Point in County Londonderry and was run by former British Army soldiers sympathetic to the Loyalist cause.

Among them were a former Royal Marine and UDA member, and Brian Nelson, who had served in the Black Watch. It later emerged that Nelson was an agent for the British Army's Force Research Unit, or FRU. He had been brought up on the Shankill and signed up at the age of 17. When he was discharged in 1969, he signed up for the UDA. Five years later he was convicted of kidnapping and sent down for seven years. On his release Nelson had a change of heart and decided that he wanted to help the army and offered his services to the FRU. He was to become a major influence on the early operations of C Company, providing a lot of the intelligence, but he was also inadvertently to help get rid of the old guard of the UDA and clear the path for me and other new blood, together known as the Young Turks, to take over.

When McMichael decided it was necessary for the UDF to be set up, there was a real fear that we were getting ready for all-out war with the IRA. His plan was to make sure that we were ready for it. Every Sunday I would volunteer to go to the military camp and take part in training. We were given military uniforms and camping gear, and taught map-reading, survival techniques and surveillance. At the end of 18 weeks, you were tested on what you had learned and from that the leadership decided if you were going to be part of the elite unit.

With Nelson one of the main players in the running of the camp, and the rest all being former armed forces men, I believe that the whole thing wasn't the idea of McMichael, but in fact the British intelligence services. They wanted to have a set of people they could call on for operations that they couldn't be seen to be carrying out themselves.

These secret training sessions lasted about four hours, although occasionally we would be taken away on exercise for the weekend. Davey Payne, from Crumlin Road Opportunities, was now back on the scene and was heavily involved in deciding who made the grade. The good news for me was that he remembered me from the youth project and made sure that I wasn't held back. Others who had been asked to try out were asked if they were prepared to put their life on the line for the UDF.

While the intelligence services were almost certainly behind the training camp, the UDF's course still enabled its leaders to sort out who were the good men who could be trusted to take on major jobs. I was at the top of their list.

At the end of the training, Andy Tyrie, the Supreme Commander of the UDA, came and oversaw a passing-out parade and presented the successful trainees with their silver or gold wings. Only one in five of those who tried out for the UDF actually made it through to the end.

There was one crucial problem with the whole thing: there were no weapons or explosives training. How were we going to take on and defeat a well-armed and trained organisation like the IRA? If they had seen what we did instead, they would have pissed themselves laughing. There were guys running about with sticks pretending they were guns and motioning like they were lobbing grenades to simulate an ambush. It was embarrassing, like kids pretending to be soldiers. That would change, though, with a change in the leadership.

4

LOSS AND GAIN

In February 1985, I received a hammer blow when my close friend Mark Rosborough was murdered. We had known each other since we were kids and for a time he had even managed our skinhead band.

The brutal way in which he died haunts me to this day. Mark, who was 21 at the time, had been out drinking at the Cavern Street Social Club and was invited back to a card game on the Lower Shankill Road. Hours later, his badly battered body was found by chance at Ballygomartin rubbish dump. At the card game was Noel McCausland, who blamed Mark for an attack on his brother in 1979 that had left him with brain damage. Mark was charged with the attack, but the charges were dropped. That made no difference to them, and that night six years later it was time for revenge.

Mark was blasted several times in the back of the head from close range, but when the gang inspected his body he was still breathing. To finish him off, they choked him with a belt, which snapped, and then a length of wire.

Even after all that, he refused to die. He only gave up when they placed a mat on his head and stood on it for a quarter of an hour. In order to cover their tracks, the body was taken to the rubbish tip, where they hoped it would be buried. It was only luck that someone spotted it. Mark was so badly disfigured that he could only be identified by his tattoos. The judge at the trial described the murder as 'subhuman' and McCausland was given a life sentence for his role in the killing. It left me numb, for Mark was a good friend and what had happened was terrible, whoever the victim.

But worse was to come for me when, a few months later, I was responsible for the death of another friend in a car crash. Along with Maurice Drumgoole and a couple of others, I spent an afternoon watching an Orange flute band play before going for a couple of drinks in a pub called the Meeting of the Waters. After that we decided to head out to a nightclub at Templepatrick in County Antrim. I'd had a few drinks but insisted that I was OK to drive. I jumped behind the wheel of the VW Beetle, with Maurice behind me and the other two piled in as well.

Everything was fine. It was raining a bit, but not too hard, as I drove up Crumlin Road, heading out towards the country and following the Horseshoe bend in the north of the city. All I can remember is losing control of the car as I took one of the tight curves. It rolled twice before ending up on the roof. As soon as it came to a stop, I looked round to see how everybody was. At a glance everything seemed to be OK. There was no blood and the car had somehow managed to escape serious damage. I remember the three of us talking, checking how we were as we clambered out of the wreck, which was still upside down. There wasn't a mark or a scrape on any of us. But Maurice was still in the back of the car. He hadn't moved. His neck was broken and he died at the scene.

The police appeared and took us to Antrim police station, where I had to tell them what had happened. I was badly shaken and was in shock for weeks afterwards. Maurice was one of my best friends and I'd been driving when he died. On 19 November 1986, I appeared at Antrim Magistrates' Court and was convicted of reckless driving while under the influence of alcohol and without insurance or a licence. It was a terrible period of my life and it was difficult to come to terms with what had happened. Maurice and I had been like brothers, and every Sunday without fail I spent an hour at his grave.

At his funeral, Maurice's family were great to me, accepting that it had been an accident and that any one of the four of us could have died. Despite this, I still felt that it was my fault. If I hadn't been at the wheel, Maurice would still be here. I was jailed for six months, banned from driving for three years and fined £150. I was bailed until my appeal hearing could be heard.

Things went from bad to worse. Sometime after the trial,

I was left fighting for my life when Sam and I were attacked by a gang of Catholics at the back of my house. To be honest, we were caught off guard because the last thing we expected was to be set upon in our own territory. It was a big risk for a gang of Republicans to come into our patch and start trouble. If they had been caught, they might well not have made it back across the peace line.

The brawl didn't last long. The gang were in and out very quickly. Although I was only stabbed once in the back, my injuries were the most serious. The blade punctured my bladder, sliced through the lung and ripped the spleen. The assault left me in hospital for weeks and the medics put my chances of pulling through at no better than 40 per cent. My family were called to the hospital and told to expect the worst. It was particularly tough for Gina, who was expecting our second child, Natalie.

Sam was very lucky and spent just one night in hospital. When a blade entered his chest, his ribs stopped it from piercing his heart. If it had gone in at a different angle, I doubt he would have made it.

Not long afterwards, I lost my appeal and was banged up in Crumlin Road. When I got out in the middle of 1987, I turned my back on work and became a full-time UDA man.

Two years earlier, Margaret Thatcher and Garret Fitzgerald, the Irish Prime Minister, had signed the Anglo-Irish Agreement at Hillsborough Castle outside Belfast. For the first time Dublin had a direct say in the running of Northern Ireland. Since then the fear that all-out war with the Provos was just around the corner had been getting worse and worse. People flocked to become members of the UDA and membership almost doubled. For me the biggest influence was Winkie Dodds, who was now running C Company. He was the man who asked me if I had the bottle to take on military operations. Up to that point I'd paid my dues and kept a low profile. I knew Winkie when I was a young kid, but it was only when he was released from prison for robbing a post office that we became close.

It wasn't long after Winkie was released that he was picked up for the shooting of Sinn Fein member Harry Fitzsimmons. That impressed me. If the cops were right, he was in among it straight away, and that proved how much he believed in the cause.

Winkie made it through the seven days of interrogation at Castlereagh. The police knew that the intelligence for the operation had come from their mole Brian Nelson. It wasn't hard for them to join up the dots, but Winkie still walked.

C Company was split into 24 teams and there were about a thousand of us in total. I was still just a rank-and-file member when, at the usual Friday-night meeting, I was called into the back room by Winkie and asked if I was prepared to get my hands dirty. He did the same with Sammy that night, the idea being that the two of us would operate together. I'd never done anything like it before, but as far as I was concerned it had reached the stage where somebody had to.

I didn't need a lot of persuasion, as I felt I could put my faith in Winkie. He wanted the same thing for the UDA as

I did, to turn it into a fighting force capable of taking on the IRA. We got on and would talk about what direction we thought the UDA should be moving in. He gave me hope that the crowd that were currently at the top could be swept away.

As military commander, Winkie's job was to pick men and targets. At this stage, Brian Nelson was the UDA's overall intelligence officer and he was securing the information on targets with the help of the FRU.

The first step was for Winkie to say that something was being planned at headquarters, then he would come to your house and run through what was to be done. Next came surveillance, preferably carried out first thing in the morning, to make sure that you had your bearings right. I knew that Winkie was a hardliner, and I trusted him.

At that stage, I had no idea why people were being picked out as targets, as that decision was being taken much higher up the tree than I was.

It was only after I stopped working at the timber yard that I was entrusted with bigger jobs for the UDA. Before that it was only minor stuff, like moving materials about.

At the yard I was picking up £90 a week, and £20 extra if I did overtime, which I thought was good money. But then I started getting involved in criminal activity with the UDA and this brought in a lot more cash. The lure of easy money carrying out armed robberies meant that I couldn't see the point in going back to the grind of manual labour. I was working 50 hours a week for a wage that was nothing compared with what I could make with the UDA. Three or four of us were going out on a job and ending up with £1,000 each. I realised very quickly that crime paid, and paid well. The UDA got their slice, although not always, and even if they did there was still plenty to go around.

It was like a job: we would get up in the morning, jump into a car, drive about and target a place to rob. It was simple work and I enjoyed it. I was making a lot of money without hurting anybody. By comparison, being trapped in a big shed all day making roof trusses had felt like a prison sentence.

One job we pulled was nearly ruined by one of my Alsatians. The gang turned up at my house to pick me up to carry out a robbery, and as we pulled away the dog chased us down the road. The rest of the guys were panicking, but I told them that there was nothing to worry about as it would give up after a couple of hundred yards and go back home.

We got to the place we were going to turn over, which wasn't far from where I lived. Everything went without a hitch. But, as I came back out to get into the getaway vehicle, the daft dog appeared, jumped up on top of me and put its paws on my shoulders.

That dog was crazy. If you left him on his own for too long, he would go for you, even if he knew you. I decided to use this to my advantage. Everywhere I went I would get stopped by the police and searched. At one stage I was getting hauled over to the side of the road almost 20 times a day, and I'd had enough.

One day I deliberately stopped at a roadblock to let the cops have a look about the car. They took my licence and then asked me to open the boot. I let the catch off, which opened it slightly, and as one officer went to lift the boot the dog sprang out. Thinking it was a gunman, the copper just about managed to cock his rifle, but the shock nearly gave him a heart attack.

By now the security services were getting wind of the fact that C Company was on the rise and began keeping close tabs on us. The first time I was pulled in for a murder was after the killing of Patrick Hamill. He was an English Catholic, originally from Leicester, who was gunned down by two Loyalist hitmen in September 1987. He had lived just off Springfield Road for five years after marrying a local woman. An inquest heard that the killers entered Hamill's house dressed in boiler suits and shot him in the head and chest. He died the next day in hospital.

The cops came and arrested me because the commander of B Company fingered me for it. He was a tout for Special Branch and needed to keep his handlers happy. He was more than happy to sacrifice any of us to keep the pressure off himself. When they got me to Castlereagh, the detectives told me they had a witness who could put me at the scene, but they were just trying to pile the pressure on me.

Brian Nelson had supplied the intelligence for the hit, but Hamill was a mistake. During questioning, the police told me that a top Provo had lived in the house before him. I was held for two days and then released.

The same gun that had been used to kill Hamill was also used in the shooting of Francisco Notarantonio in west Belfast in October 1987. I wasn't pulled in for it but it was a very significant and controversial hit by Loyalist gunmen.

As with most of the operations carried out by C Company at this stage, the intelligence was supplied by the FRU's agent Brian Nelson. It emerged later on that on this occasion, Nelson slipped up and handed over the details of the security services' best Republican mole, codenamed Stakeknife, who lived a few doors from Notarantonio in Ballymurphy.

At the last minute, the target was changed from Stakeknife to the 66-year-old retired taxi driver and former IRA man. Gunmen broke into Notarantonio's home early in the morning and shot him dead in his bed. It's said that Stakeknife was later spotted at his funeral. Gerry Adams complained that he was amazed that a Loyalist hit squad was able to get in and out of the area without being picked up, despite the fact that the area was crawling with army personnel.

Successes like this were down to Nelson and his handlers. Whenever he was involved, C Company gunmen got a clear run in and out of Republican areas. His handlers knew that Loyalist gunmen had balls, but not the information that they needed. The Provisionals were causing mayhem but there was little that the people at the top were able to do, so they looked elsewhere. The FRU probably knew who Nelson was giving the intelligence to, but they had no intention of stopping it.

5

HEROES AND TRAITORS

Michael Stone was given life sentences for each of the three mourners he killed during his cold-blooded attack at Milltown Cemetery in March 1988. Like most viewers, I watched stunned as the television cameras caught the bearded hitman moving between the headstones to launch his one-man assault on Republicans attending the funeral of three IRA bombers shot dead by the SAS on Gibraltar. Neither his name nor his face meant anything to me before he embarked on his seemingly suicidal mission to kill Sinn Fein leaders Gerry Adams and Martin McGuinness.

To me, and plenty of other young Loyalists at the time, the media images of Stone heralded the start of a new era in our fight against the IRA and their supporters. He wasn't a criminal, but a hero. The relationship between the two of us has soured since then, but that does not take away from the impact it had on me and volunteers like me.

If Stone had succeeded in killing the leaders of Sinn Fein and the alleged leaders of the IRA, it would have been a devastating blow to the whole movement. Even though he ultimately failed in his brazen attack, he still became an inspiration to Loyalists all over Northern Ireland. I was so impressed by what he had done that I made it my mission to visit him when he started his sentence at the Maze.

What Stone did astounded me. There was no way I would have attempted anything like that. I wouldn't have had the nerve. The first I heard about it was when it flashed up on the TV news. To be honest, I was glad that one of our own was hitting back. More importantly, it reassured young volunteers like me that there were people in the UDA who were more than part-timers and who weren't in the pockets of Special Branch. Stone had been prepared to take on an operation of this size with no support or back-up.

I have no doubt he knew that, had the IRA got their hands on him, there would have been little chance they wouldn't have killed him quickly. Three days later, at the funeral service for Kevin Brady, one of Stone's three victims, the IRA showed little mercy towards two army corporals. Derek Wood, 24, and David Howes, 23, had driven into the funeral cortege and were dragged out of their VW Passat as they tried to leave the scene. After being battered and thrown over a high wall, the pair were bundled into the back of a waiting taxi and driven to waste ground near Penny Lane. Corporal Wood was shot six times and stabbed four times in the back of the neck. Corporal Howes was shot five times. Stone would have been afforded even less dignity.

As I watched the pictures of the Milltown incident, I was in awe of the cold and calm way Stone went about it. He made no effort to protect his identity and remained cool throughout the attack. At one point he dropped his hat, but was focused enough to stop and pick it up. At first I thought he must be an undercover soldier, with back-up hidden about the cemetery. It was hard to believe it was a one-man operation. Only when he started throwing the grenades and firing indiscriminately was I convinced that he was a paramilitary.

When it emerged that the gunman was Michael Stone, a young Loyalist from east Belfast, he became an immediate inspiration to many who wanted to take on the IRA. But not everybody felt the same way, and the killings sent shivers through the leadership of the UDA. The first thing they did was to deny that they had any idea what Stone had been planning, or even that they knew who he was.

Instead of celebrating what he had done, they turned their backs on him. It confirmed what we all knew: that they had no stomach for the fight. The problem was that there was an agreement between the IRA and the UDA that the leaders of both movements were immune from attack. Stone had decisively ended that.

The UDA were so desperate to wash their hands of him that they told anyone who would listen that he must have been on drugs to have tried what he did. To me and other young volunteers, the treatment of Stone was shameful. He was a hero to us. Here was a man who went to Milltown Cemetery knowing that there was a good chance he would be killed or, if not, spend the rest of his life behind bars.

As it turned out, everything had changed by the time he was ready to start his sentence in the Maze. The UDA and the UVF were falling over themselves to get him on their wing in the prison and adopt him as their hero. In the end, the UDA got their way, and through a friend I managed to arrange a visit. I was so proud that Michael Stone had allowed me to visit him. You could give cash to an official at the prison to pass on to the lags, so I signed Michael Stone in £20; it was the very least that I could do for a hero of the Loyalist movement.

I remember leaving the prison and feeling inspired. Still a relatively inexperienced volunteer, I admired Stone's courage and commitment. Some people think it is wrong to celebrate what he did, but those were the circumstances of the time. Stone's actions rocked the heart of the Republican movement and made him a legend overnight.

Less than a year later, Republican lawyer Pat Finucane was gunned down as he and his family were having a Sunday meal. During that period I'd moved through the ranks and, by 12 February 1989, when Finucane was killed, the cops had me down as the rising star of the UDA. They were tipped off that I'd done the murder, but they wouldn't have needed much convincing.

The fact was that I had no knowledge of the Finucane murder before it happened. As with the Stone killings, the first I knew about it was when it was on the television news.

A sledgehammer gang smashed their way through Finucane's front door and the gunmen unleashed 14 shots from a revolver and a pistol, all of which hit him. His wife was also hit, but only in the foot. The UFF released a statement claiming responsibility for the killing. It said they had shot 'Pat Finucane the Provisional IRA officer, not Pat Finucane the solicitor'.

There is no doubt that Finucane and his family were staunch Republicans. His brother John was in the IRA and killed in a car crash while on active service. Another brother had been the fiancee of Mairead Farrell, one of the three IRA activists shot dead on Gibraltar by the SAS. Finucane had also appeared on behalf of high-profile Republicans such as hunger strikers Bobby Sands and Pat McGeown.

The authorities were also certain that in 1980 Finucane had smuggled guns into Crumlin Road Prison for IRA prisoners, where they were in the middle of a trial for the murder of SAS soldier Herbert Westmacott. The screws hated the lawyer with a passion, and one said to me, 'That bastard comes in here and doesn't even look us in the eye.'

To cap it all, three weeks before Finucane was killed, junior Home Office Minister Douglas Hogg told the House of Commons, 'I have to state as a fact, but with great regret, that there are a number of solicitors in Northern Ireland who are unduly sympathetic to the cause of the IRA.' It was as good as an invitation. Finucane's importance to the Republican movement was clear, and that made him a legitimate target.

I was at home when the cops came to take me to

Castlereagh. Despite their belief they had got their man, the interrogation was a breeze, the easiest I ever had in Castlereagh. Any other time I was held there, they played the long game, gave you nothing, broke you down slowly. But this time I was given cups of tea and allowed to smoke, which was as good as it was ever going to get in there. The reason? They were delighted that Finucane was dead. They detested him. All of them.

While I was sitting in the interrogation cell, other detectives kept coming in and congratulating me as the man who had 'done Pat the rat'. One cop in particular came in and thanked me. With a big smile on his face, he said that as soon as he heard what had happened he threw open his drinks cabinet and got drunk. Others were saying, 'It's the best hit the UFF has ever done.'

It was also the first time that I came across Jonty Brown, the officer who would later claim responsibility for having me locked up for directing terrorism. I remember exactly how he first introduced himself. He said, 'Detective Sergeant Brown, head of the murder squad, north Belfast, Antrim Road. I'm here to question you about the murder of Patrick Finucane.' The interview was to run on over seven days.

C Company's Jackie Thompson and Winkie Dodds, were in with me for the duration as well. But it was nothing to do with us. As far as I know, it was down to B Company, which was why we were now in the frame.

What nobody else knew was that on the day Finucane was murdered Jackie Thompson was locked up in Crumlin Road Prison doing five days for an unpaid fine. And Jackie kept his mouth shut. For two days he let the cops interrogate him about Finucane and played along, saying nothing about his alibi. So it was all the sweeter when they checked with the prison authorities. They had blown it, and, worse than that, Jackie was taking the piss out of them as well. Of course, our innocence made no difference and they kept us locked up for seven days anyway.

Finucane's murder had been choreographed from the top. It was a good hit and a legitimate one. However, it was wrong that the British intelligence services were pulling the strings in the background, and, more importantly, that they would have happily sat back and watched as the wrong person went to prison for it.

The collusion between the security forces and Loyalists in the killing of Finucane would be investigated by the Deputy Chief Constable of Cambridgeshire, John Stevens, who would play a major role in clearing the decks of the UDA old guard. He had first been called in following the murder of Loughlin Maginn at Rathfriland in County Down on 25 August 1989.

Loyalist gunmen had burst into Maginn's home on the Lissize Estate and opened fire, hitting him in the hand, arm and chest as he tried to make his escape. Maginn, 28, was the fourth Catholic to be killed in the first six months of that year, and it also emerged that he had been complaining about harassment by the security forces before being gunned down. The UFF were put under pressure to prove that Maginn, whose uncle was an SDLP councillor, had paramilitary connections. What happened next was to set in motion a domino effect that would clear out the old leadership and open the door for new blood like me to come through.

Documents were produced which said that Maginn was an IRA intelligence officer. The trouble was that they were classified and sent a message to the Nationalist movement that there was collusion between the British security services and Loyalist paramilitaries. And in March 1992 two UDR soldiers, Andrew Browne and Andrew Smith, were given life sentences for passing on the information that led to Maginn's death. Two UFF members from Lisburn, Geoffrey McCullough and Edward Jones, also received life.

These revelations of collusion and leaked documents caused a massive outcry and the authorities' response was to call in Stevens. The result of his investigation was the outing of UDA intelligence boss Brian Nelson as a member of the FRU, working for the army. The word was that Nelson had provided gunmen with vital details on dozens of operations that had gone off without a hitch. Despite this, he was given only ten years.

On completion of his task, Stevens had charged almost 60 paramilitaries on both sides and succeeded in getting rid of the deadwood. Tommy 'Tucker' Lyttle, the west Belfast commander, and his son were also his victims. Meanwhile, John McMichael had been blown up by the IRA in December 1987, Andy Tyrie had walked away after finding a bomb under his car not long after and Davey Payne was behind bars after being caught with the Lebanese AK-47s.

That left the way almost clear for the Young Turks to take

control of the UDA and transform it from a bunch of racketeering nobodies into an efficient organisation capable of opposing the IRA. There was just one more obstacle.

Katherine Spruce was someone I'd got involved with who quickly became trouble. The RUC and intelligence services were getting more and more concerned about me and they wanted to use Spruce as a supergrass. She was the first woman to become a headline informer in their battle to bring me down.

They hoped to build a case against me, Skelly, Jackie Thompson and Tommy Irvine that would show we were a sectarian murder gang who crossed the peace line and murdered Catholics just for the sake of it. They said there was no targeting, just random killing. Katherine Spruce was to be a major part of their plan. I first met her not long after she moved into the Oldpark area, a couple of hundred yards from where I lived. She came over to my car after recognising me and said that she knew all about me. One thing led to another and we had an affair. When Gina found out, she walked out on me. I got myself a new flat and for a short time Spruce lived there with me.

She was a kind, decent person, but completely off her head. I became her obsession, and it was a full-on affair. It was only the second time I met her that I realised how she felt. After removing her jeans, she took off her knickers to reveal a tattoo of my name in big, black, inky letters. I knew then that she was a bit special. I mean, she didn't even know me.

It soon became a nightmare. All she wanted to do was

spend her money on me, and she would leave messages on the blackboard for me directing me to where the latest gift had been stashed. That doesn't sound all that bad, but it was torture. She just wanted me more and more, until I got sick of her.

It went on longer than it should have because there was another side of our relationship that was beneficial to me. She had been in a relationship with IPLO man Martin 'Rook' O'Prey. That meant she could get into places I had no chance of going to. There her eyes and ears picked up good intelligence that let me know what the other side was getting up to. Her pals had no idea that she was seeing me, so there was no suspicion and nothing was held back. O'Prey was shot dead in 1991 when UVF gunmen burst into his house.

In the end, though, Spruce was driving me nuts and I decided no amount of information could make it worth putting up with her. It didn't go down well. When I told her it was over, at first she thought I was making it up. Then it sank in. It had got to the stage where she had fallen in love with me and she wasn't going to let it go. On and on she pestered me until someone had to tell her to get out of the area. Then she went to the police. They couldn't believe their luck when this golden opportunity to get me locked up just walked in the door.

On the surface, all they had was a complaint that she had been forced to move out of her home, but the detectives realised that they had Johnny Adair's ex and she could be squeezed for all sorts of information. They were desperate to get me off the streets, and the embittered woman in front of them was the key. Between them they managed to come up with three attempted murders of Republicans that they could charge me with.

The first was former Sinn Fein councillor Sean Keenan, who had been shot by the UFF in June 1990. The team of hitmen parked their vehicle at the side of the M1 motorway and made their way to his house on Riverdale Park South in Andersonstown. Disguised as soldiers on foot patrol, they went unchallenged. In full combats and camouflage, they were able to walk through the heart of Republican west Belfast without a hitch.

After entering, having attacked the house at the rear, where a weakness in the security had been identified, the gunmen found Keenan watching television. When he realised what was happening, he bolted upstairs, but as he fled a round caught him in the leg. The Republican newspaper *An Phoblacht* reported that the men had carried out the raid with 'military precision'. It was also the second time that Keenan had escaped with his life: he had previously been shot while travelling in a car with Gerry Adams.

Spruce and the RUC also claimed that C Company had tried to execute Edward 'The Sugarman' McKinney, from Atlantic Avenue in north Belfast, on 8 May and John McGuinness on 5 July 1990. They also threw in charges of a kneecapping, membership of the UFF and possession of guns when they arrested us in August of that year.

While I was locked up, a Catholic called Dermot McGuinness was shot dead on Rosapenna Street as he walked home. Witnesses said that gunmen tried to force him into a car and when he refused they shot him six times. The UFF claimed responsibility and said that 41-year-old McGuinness was a member of the IPLO, but this was rejected by his family. The car used in the murder was dumped outside my house, which the RUC duly searched inch by inch. The attack had been nothing to do with me and the vehicle was left there to say to the police that I could not have everything pinned on me.

The murder of McGuinness came just minutes after the IRA gunned down Stephen Craig outside the Chester Park Hotel in Belfast. The 24-year-old Protestant had left the police six months before he was killed and was waiting for a taxi when he was shot. That's the reality of what was going on.

Spruce told the police that while we were having a relationship she had heard about the operations and had even provided support. She gave them a 13-page statement and in the opening lines said that she had known me for more than ten years and we'd had a child together. It was total nonsense, and I could prove it. The cops charged us on that basis, but I knew there was no way in a million years it was going to stick.

So desperate were they to believe what Spruce had to say that they didn't stop for a second to question the truth of what she claimed. A blood test would prove that I wasn't a father of any child, and that would destroy any credibility that she had, though one was never taken in the end. She even told the police that we kept our guns in holsters like something out of a cowboy movie. Spruce had assisted in putting together a case against us by using what few personal details she knew and from watching the news on the television. Her story didn't add up. She couldn't keep the show going and the cops knew it. After four months on remand the charges were dropped in December 1990. The RUC were furious that the case had collapsed. But, during the time they had kept us off the streets, sectarian murders in north and west Belfast had more or less come to a halt.

As for Spruce, she was promised the earth by the detectives and then, when the case collapsed, she was cut adrift, which was what they were always going to do to her. When we walked free she phoned me from police protective custody saying that she was going to sue them. She was raging that they were keeping her locked up. I told her that was what they did with informers who had passed their sell-by date and that he RUC abandon you when you're no longer any use to them, and I put the phone down. It was the last time I heard from her.

6

NEW BLOOD

It wasn't just the RUC who were surprised when the charges against the four of us were dropped. C Company's leaders were convinced that we were going away for a very long time and effectively turned their back on us. It was the last mistake they would make.

Sammy Verner and his son, Sam junior, were old-style UDA men who had little interest in anything other than making money out of the Langley Street Social Club. As well as being a regular haunt for C Company men, the place was supposed to be a source of income for the cause. The Verners claimed that it hardly broke even.

I first noticed their attitude when I was taken in for questioning about the Finucane murder and they had little interest at all in what was going on. Normally, when someone was locked up, the rest of the company would rally round, make sure that he had everything that he needed. The Verners bothered more about when they were going to get their dues.

When I was remanded on the Spruce-related charges it was even worse. They were sure that I was going to jail for at least 25 years. There was no sign of the trainers and jeans that were usually sent up to guys on remand. For four months I sat there and stewed over the way they were treating us. It wasn't good enough. I was the one taking risks, desperate to go to war with the IRA, while they sat in Langley Street watching the club's bank balance get bigger. Things had to change.

On the day we walked free, C Company was reborn and we never looked back. A meeting was arranged, to be held in the upstairs room of Langley Street, and all the local commanders and their staff were told to be there. Before anything happened the main men were sounded out about the coup. Most of them were behind the plan, but there were those who were concerned what would happen if the Verners resisted. It made no difference: they had to go.

In the end they scarcely put up a fight. A team walked into the room and told them their time was up and they should leave straight away. The pair of them were having none of it to begin with, but when guns were produced they soon changed their minds. Warning shots were fired above their heads and into the ground. They were allowed to walk out. A new order was in place and more than a hundred people watched as the coup swept away the old regime. It was the beginning of a new era.

NEW BLOOD

There was already a good group of men in place at the centre who were willing to give their all to the cause and get their hands dirty. But there was a long way to go, for the reality was that C Company was in a sorry state and would have to work to be in a position to take on the Republicans. At least now there was an opportunity for us to reinvent the organisation and give ourselves a chance to score victories against the Nationalists. Men kept coming forward to offer any help they could, but first we had to restructure and ensure that, most importantly of all, the flow of money was increased. Racketeering and extortion scams had to be made more efficient and their scale increased.

I aimed to get a team of men at the top of C Company who could be trusted and wanted to push the Loyalist movement forward in the same direction as I did. Sam 'Skelly' McCrory, Jackie Thompson, Donald Hodgen and another man I'll call Mac (name changed for reasons of security) were all appointed to be on its staff. Between them they covered the roles of second in command, military commander and provost marshal. I'd grown up with most of them on the Shankill and I knew that I could trust them. For those who joined up that I didn't know, the test of their loyalty would come inside the walls of Castlereagh. If they made it through seven days of interrogation, I knew that I could trust them.

The staff would get together daily to discuss how C Company was going to move forward, select targets and look at the latest intelligence. Our information was gathered from all sorts of sources, the best coming from the British Army.

I was able to strike up a good relationship with a lot of soldiers because many of the squaddies saw us as fighting the same war and them. That meant they were happy to let us know what they did. I would be stopped at security checkpoints many times every day and that was the best time to see what the latest developments were. Normally in every patrol there would be three or four squaddies who were friendly to me. When I was stopped, I would be taken out of the car and searched. To make sure they didn't get caught out handing me intelligence, I was walked to the back of the car to watch a dummy root about in the boot. There the information was passed over, unseen by any soldiers who didn't agree with what they were doing.

I would get to know what type of cars the Republicans were driving, where they were being spotted hanging about and if they were using a safe house. Every day before the troops went on to the streets their officer in command would make sure they knew the very latest intelligence. During the briefing there was little mention of Loyalists because they knew we were on their side.

However, at the end of one meeting my name did come up. According to one squaddie, just as they were about to go out of the door the OC produced a mugshot of me and scoffed, 'Last but not least, Mr Adair. He is active in this area and it might be an idea to have a word with him. We are supposed to be helping the RUC.' The rest of the soldiers fell about the place laughing. It will seem like nothing more than a cynical ploy to some, but I did everything I could to let the troops know that we supported them. The squaddies realised that the Loyalist paramilitaries were on their side, and, unlike the IRA, we weren't trying to blow them up.

On 3 August 1992 Scots Guard Damian Shackleton was shot dead by the IRA while travelling in the back of a Land Rover patrol in the New Lodge area. The 21-year-old's patrol had just turned into Duncairn Avenue when a sniper opened fire from the flat they had taken over close by. Later I heard how another soldier held him as he died and was genuinely moved. I went personally to his barracks and handed over a wreath signed by me and everyone at C Company.

Much as they were the enemy, I knew that the IRA were a very good organisation, and grudgingly I respected them. I also knew that we could take lessons from them and play them at their own game. Their armoury and their tactics had to become ours.

Until the Young Turks took over, C Company's strike rate had been embarrassing. Nine times out of ten a unit that was sent out to launch an attack on someone's house wasn't getting over the threshold because the doors were reinforced with steel. Making a noise at the front door and firing a few rounds into the air wasn't good enough.

The IRA met with the same problem when they came on to our patch, so they adapted their tactics, taking over houses and waiting for the mark to appear. I saw this and realised it was the way forward. It took a lot of bottle to sit armed behind enemy lines, but it was far better than driving in, firing off a few rounds and leaving. The bottom line was that our men were no different from the IRA gunmen, and there was no reason why they couldn't carry out the same missions. If C Company could bring terror to the doors of active Republicans, they were going to have to sit up and think.

A lot of the intelligence was also gathered by ourselves and in a variety of different ways. Belfast was a divided city, not just on religious grounds but also physically. Protestants lived in the Shankill area and Catholics in the Ardoyne and Falls. To find out what was going on beyond the peace line meant you had to go into enemy territory and that was never an easy job. I used a number of different ruses that would allow me to move about places like the Ardoyne without anyone thinking I wasn't supposed to be there.

The easiest way to get around it was to wear a Celtic shirt. People assume that I'm a big Rangers supporter, but I could barely name a player. What I did know was that with the green and white of Celtic on I had a better chance of moving about unchallenged. Cars and faces that didn't look right would be viewed with suspicion straight away. But with the right shirt on and a Celtic pennant in the car it was much easier. It was so good that I had the confidence to go into a pub on the Falls Road, order a pint and see who was coming and going. It ended up becoming a fashion thing for Protestant kids, who would buy Celtic shirts and get 'Johnny Adair – Simply the Best' printed on the back just to noise up the Catholics.

When I noticed that lurchers were very popular in the Ardoyne, I borrowed a couple and would take them for a walk first thing in the morning to see what was going on.

Top: Me with Sam Skelly and drummer Julian 'Tarzan' Carson acknowledging the applause at a gig on the Shankill in 1982.

Bottom: As a teenager.

Bottom pic: Photopress, Belfast

Top left: As a kid. I'm in the tank top.

Top right: As a teenager

Bottom left: With Stevie McKeag months before he died.

Bottom right: Inside the Maze with Sam 'Skelly' McCroy and a replica gun.

Top: With Michael Stone at a Loyalist rally, August 2000.

Bottom: At a Drumcree protest in July 2000

Press Eye Ltd, Belfast

Top left: Walking out of Maghaberry Prison, May 2002.

Top right: Champagne to celebrate my release.

Bottom: With Gina at welcome home party.

Press Eye Ltd, Belfast

The scene of devastation outside the Shankill fish shop in October 1993. An IRA bomb meant for me exploded early.

Photopress, Belfast

Top: Gina in her wedding dress before setting off to jail to marry me in the Maze prison. Bridesmaid Natalie is on the left and Chloe, her flowergirl, on the right, February 1997.

Bottom: Me and Gina with the kids, early 1990s.

Former RUC Detective Sergeant Johnston Brown, who was subject of an attempted murder inside The John Hewitt Bar in Lower Donegal Street in Belfast in February 2005. Jonty was the man who claimed the glory for jailing me.

Top: Gunmen appear at the bonfire at the Drumcree protest, July 2000.

Bottom: Members of the UFF announce to the press that they have appointed a representative to meet General John de Chastelain to discuss decommissioning.

Before the IRA knew who I was, I could stroll around pretty freely. And when I got my hands on a black taxi I would drive about keeping an eye on things. It would be loaded up with female passengers and kids to help us blend in. There was also a supply of clean cars to move about in. They belonged to people that the police had no knowledge of and so they wouldn't set off alarm bells when the number plate was checked. Using your own car wasn't an option. The Republicans knew my car registration and the details were painted on the walls to warn people. All this had to be done without being armed, because if the RUC found a weapon on you it would be straight to prison. I was never caught when I was on reconnaissance but there were a couple of close shaves.

Once I was stopped by a team from the RUC's D Division as I was taking UFF volunteer Ricky Calderwood back to the Maze. D Division were an elite section who specialised in keeping tabs on known terrorist suspects and were briefed every day. They would know what kind of car I was driving, who I'd been spotted with, anything that might help them track me down. It was the usual questions: where have you been? Where are you going? How long are you going to be?

There was one copper who was always on my tail and liked trying to give me a hard time. A few days earlier, the UFF had admitted responsibility for a murder and he decided to have a go at me, saying the hit had been sloppy and there was no way I would boast about it in front of him and his team. I gave him what he wanted and shouted at him that the operation had been a success. He was even more embarrassed when I added, 'Fair play to the UFF,' and he had to let me go.

Driving back from the prison a couple of hours later, I found the Crumlin Road covered in roadblocks, so I decided to cut through the Ardoyne. Still smarting from earlier on, that copper and his team spotted me and followed me. Looking in the mirror I thought I'd lost them but the Jeep cut across the front of my car and I was stopped outside the Shamrock Club, a regular IRA haunt. The copper was in dreamland; it couldn't have worked out better for him.

Walking towards the driver's door of my car, he started yelling, 'Get out of the car, Johnny.' A guy was standing in the doorway of the pub watching what was going on. He didn't know who I was but the cops were making sure that anyone within a five-mile radius could hear my name. 'Over here, Johnny,' was the next command, drawing me closer to the pub so that everyone could see me. 'What's wrong with you now, Johnny? You're not mouthing off about the UFF now?' came the next instalment. He might as well have drawn a target on my back. I was shaking and my legs were like jelly, but I continued to be cocky.

It was the middle of the afternoon and the schools had just finished. Looking away from the police and glancing up the street, I noticed that there were mums and their kids coming down the hill. It was only a matter of time before they realised who I was. It wasn't looking good. If the women got involved the men would be out of the pub like a shot. One of the women shouted, 'That's Johnny Adair. He's always in here snooping about.'

I thought my best chance was just to blank it and say I was a Catholic and I was getting harassed by the police patrol. It didn't work and the women started trying to get past the soldiers, who were part of the patrol as well, to spit on me and hit me. The cops were laughing their heads off as they were quite happy to sit back and watch me be fed to the lions. Mercifully, the soldiers kept them back, but, if the scene had got out of control and the men had come out, there was little chance I would have made it back to the Shankill.

Realising things were about to get out of hand, the copper who had it in for me shouted, 'Right, Johnny, you can go now.' As I turned to walk back to the car, he tossed my licence on to the roof and bellowed, 'Don't forget your paperwork, Mr Adair.'

I got behind the wheel as fast as I could and sped away before the crowd got their hands on me. The cops even charged me with breach of the peace over what happened.

If I, or the others, hadn't had the bottle to go into places like the Ardoyne and have a sniff about, none of the operations would ever have got off the ground. It was risky enough for an ASU to move about the city, so it was important that they weren't wasting their time on a place which was too well defended. It was also a good plan to find out where the target parked their car. Was it ditched around the corner or left at the door?

In the early days the teams would be sent out in the

middle of the night. The drawback was that it was likely that their car would be the only one on the move at that time and more likely to be remembered.

Our security and dedication to ensuring that plans weren't compromised was also a top priority. On any operation only the military commander would be trusted with advance knowledge of what was going on. The team would only be told what was happening right at the last minute. A dummy run was often used to make sure that the driver knew where he was going, where to stop and how to make his getaway. If the ASU wasn't fully trusted they would only be told hours before the hit was to take place, normally in a safe house.

When it was time to move, the team would be given boiler suits or a set of new clothes, the plan was double-checked and they were told where the safe house was after the operation had gone down. At the last minute, the weapons were handed over. They were always tested in the days leading up to the operation. There was no need to go to the countryside to make sure they were working; they would be fired in estates on the Shankill. It wasn't unusual to hear the crack of a gun being discharged at night. People knew that, if they heard 30 shots and there was nothing on the news, the chances were that C Company was trying out new guns.

Before any operation, the team met and talked through the plan. For days beforehand, the nerves would burn the inside of your stomach. There would be plenty of sleepless nights spent tossing and turning as you went over and over what was going to happen. Once they were on the road the unit quickly forgot about the nerves and concentrated on the job in hand. If everything went according to plan, there would be a prearranged meeting at a safe house. The car would be dumped and the men involved would burn their clothes and have a bath to get rid of any forensic trace.

Normally, the team would sit tight for a couple of days until the heat died down. It was a very strict procedure and if it wasn't followed the cops would probably track you down. The fewer people who knew about an operation, the less chance there was of going to jail.

The UFF claimed responsibility for any operations that we carried out through the media. A password would be said to the selected reporter and the details would be passed on. Propaganda was key to letting fellow Protestants know that we weren't going to sit back and watch as the IRA slaughtered our people.

When the Verners had been in charge, the armoury was a shambles. In general, the Loyalist movement was very poorly armed. To my knowledge there was only ever one successful shipment of Loyalist weapons that made it to the shores of Ulster, and that was in 1987. The deal was funded by a £300,000 bank robbery in Portadown and the guns were brought in hidden under £5,000 worth of ceramic tiles. The plan was that, after clearing customs, they would be divided between the UDA, UVF and Ulster Resistance. The cargo was over 200 AK-47s, 90 Browning 9mm pistols, 500 anti-personnel grenades, RPG7 rocket launchers and tens of thousands of rounds of ammunition.

The problem for the UDA was that Davey Payne got caught with our share.

The extent of the Verners' C Company armoury was an old .45 revolver and a double-barrelled shotgun. Without guns and bullets the whole thing was a total waste of time. How were we going to fight the IRA with two guns? The only other source of guns was burglars who nicked them from cops and sold them to us. But it wasn't good enough to just rely on hoods who knocked over homes.

Over a period of six months to a year, C Company was able to secure a sophisticated collection of hardware that included RPG7s, AK-47s, automatic handguns, hand grenades and machine guns. Through contacts in the London underworld, a supply line was set up to make sure that we were well stocked up. There were no massive shipments: most of the time the guns would be stashed in the door panels of cars that had been bought at auction. Three or four cars would make the trip together and bring back the weapons.

There was also a supply line from Scotland. It was very small, with just the occasional bit of hardware coming over from Stranraer, but it was steady. Cairnryan, near Stranraer, was also used for a time, although one person was nabbed there with five handguns.

Ulster Resistance made sure that C Company was properly armed. They were a shadowy movement made up of prominent members of society who didn't want to actually get their hands dirty but were happy to make sure that we were fit to go. Their ranks were filled with prison officers, landowners, RUC men, even the clergy. Although they weren't going to go on operations, Ulster Resistance snapped up their slice of the 1987 shipment in case of a doomsday situation. C Company was able to strike up a relationship with them and tap into their stocks. The more success we had, the happier Ulster Resistance were to hand over guns.

There was also a large supply of homemade weapons which were put together at Harland and Wolff shipyard or Shorts aviation factory. They weren't identical to Uzis or machine guns, nor as accurate, but the 'spitters' were still deadly.

Deactivated weapons were popular as well. A guy in England was buying them for £90, doing his stuff and then selling them on for between £600 and £1,200, depending on what kind of gun it was. Something wasn't right about it, though. C Company bought £30,000 worth of them and every single one of them ended up in the hands of the RUC.

Weapons such as assault rifles were like gold dust and so had to be handled very carefully. C Company had guns oiled, greased and buried out in the countryside. The unit was so active that guns were being used almost every day of the week and there wasn't always the time to go back and forward to the country to get them. Doing this also increased the likelihood of the police catching you. For this reason there were safe houses in the city, and at one of these lived two OAPs who would do anything for me without question. They were both in their seventies but didn't care about the risks they were taking. For me it was the perfect cover. No cops were going to look twice at them but they were up to their necks in it.

C Company was the only Loyalist group to acquire and use a rocket launcher. Nobody was killed in any of the three attacks with it, but the fact that we had got our hands on an RPG7 with warheads to go with it showed that we meant business. The security forces were very nervous about our having it. Every time it was used, a massive house-to-house search of the Shankill was undertaken to try to find it, but each time C Company made sure that it was long gone before they turned up. As soon as it was used, a team collected it and drove it more than 20 miles away, out of the reach of the RUC. The rest of the armoury was hidden all over the place. To keep the arms stored as safely as possible, C Company made a point of picking people who were whiter than white and had no links to the movement.

As C Company became more successful and our reputation grew, people were lining up to help. The support came from right across our community, not just from those who were living at the sharp end. Businessmen donated cash or helped out with military logistics. Teenagers would help with intelligence gathering or legwork.

A guy installed a CCTV camera in our security system, and when he was there he offered me further valuable assistance. He had security clearance and was able to get top-quality intelligence for C Company. In particular, he could check out car registrations – who the owners were and where they lived – and this allowed houses to be targeted. It was an example of how people wanted to impress me, and at the same time were willing to do what they could to help.

NEW BLOOD

My house had to be turned into Fort Knox. There were steel shutters protecting the windows at the front and the back of the house, and the same behind the exterior doors. The frames were reinforced and the doors fitted with a quarter-inch steel plate to stop bullets coming through. The only way in through either door was to actually remove the brick work around it and the cops did it on more than one occasion. I had dogs as well as observation lights that sent out a bright beam if anyone wandered close to the house. The windows were bombproof. It cost thousands and was all paid for out of the organisation's kitty. C Company's main men were given the same security.

From the front my home looked like a normal house but the coppers came prepared. I was getting arrested so often that it got to the stage where I would wake up at 5.30am and wait for them to smash through my front door. I would get up, have a cigarette and give it until 6am. If they hadn't shown up by then, it was OK for me to go back to bed.

Before breaking the door down, they would position a team of men at both the front of the house and the back, to block any potential escape routes. I knew the rest of the procedure by heart. Once they had battered their way in, the warrant for my arrest under the Prevention of Terrorism Act would be read out. This allowed them to lift anyone they thought was a terrorist without giving them any reason or saying what they were accused of. The house would be turned upside down, with nothing left untouched. Obviously everyone in the house would be woken up and the kids would have to be taken aside by the cops.

It wasn't just the Nationalists who got a hard time from the RUC. The cops would drill holes in the wall and stick optic lenses into the cavity to see if I'd tried to hide anything. It was all part of the game. They knew there was no way I was going to have anything in the house that could land me in the dock, but that wasn't going to stop them. They did everything possible to disrupt my life in the hope that I would take my eye off the ball.

Dressed from head to toe in forensic suits, they would work their way around the house taking samples with swabs in the hope of finding some residue from a bomb or a gun. Anywhere I would have put my hand down would be tested. The security was breached once. A hood called McBride got into the house and managed to make off with a hi-fi and a video, along with a few other things. While the house had every bit of security going, a lot of the time I didn't bother to lock the doors or windows. I was the laugh of the neighbourhood because McBride had managed to get in while I was lying in bed and I hadn't even noticed.

Castlereagh Holding Centre became a big part of my life and I was on first-name terms with most of the cops there. As prominent paramilitaries, C Company's members were taken in for questioning every other week. I would even be used to freak out any Republican prisoners who were in for questioning. Every now and then, if a Provo gunman was getting grilled by detectives, they would open the door of the interview room and get me to stick my head round the corner to say hello. It never happened the other way round.

If a guard was giving me a hard time, I would do

everything in my power to make life as difficult as possible for him. That could mean, if they took away my clothes to be analysed for gun residue, refusing to wear prison clothes and being locked up in the nude or just boxer shorts. It might not seem that important but anything to get under their skin was worth a go.

Castlereagh was also where I came into contact with Jonty Brown the most. He took every opportunity to see what made me tick. He didn't interview me every time I was banged up, but always made a point of sticking his head in to see how the interrogation was going. It felt like the loneliest place on the planet. There was nobody to hold your hand: it was you on your own against the peelers. There was no hatred between Brown and I. He would grudgingly say to me, 'You're a soldier and I'm a police officer.' As far as I was concerned, he was a good copper. It was little things that made the difference. Prisoners were allowed to smoke when they were being interviewed but it was up to the coppers. Unlike most of the others, Brown always made sure that there were cigarettes there for you, and even brought in biscuits to try to soften you up even more. He would comment on the efficiency of operations and tell me how well they were run; obviously it was another way of trying to get me onside.

Others tried their best to get in your face and play the hard man. There would be no actual physical abuse, just screaming, shouting and throwing chairs about the interview room. As soon as they started chucking their weight about, I would stonewall them. There was no way that I was going to entertain that lot. They would get frustrated they were getting nowhere and eventually let it get to them. I'm sure that the Provisionals got it worse than me. They were targeting police stations, soldiers, anything British, and that was bound to make the interrogators go at them harder.

At least once a month when the cash was flowing, I made sure that everyone got a night out. Strippers would be put on, and there would be free drink all day. I needed them to feel like they belonged to the movement and that there was an overall plan that involved them. Up until then the men had handed over their cash to the UDA and that was it. Now they were at least getting something in return, and when they watched the news at night and saw a report on how C Company had carried out an attack they could be proud to be part of what was going on.

7
EYES AND EARS

It was an article in the *Guardian* in the early 90s that gave me my nickname. Maggie O'Kane wrote, 'The police call him Mad Dog and the IRA will probably kill him.' Somehow the name stuck. By then C Company was reorganised and properly armed and taking on the Republicans. And until I was jailed in May 1994 the UDA would be my life every single hour of every single day.

But it wasn't as simple as going after the IRA: the battle was on three fronts. As well as the Nationalist terrorists, I had to take on the security services and also fight the internal struggle within the Loyalist movement. Each had to be dealt with properly: one slip-up and I'd be dead or locked up for a long time. The stronger C Company became the more challenges came our way. Now we were targets for assassination bids, approaches from Special Branch and traitors. We were all in the firing line now.

On 10 October 1991, C Company's Harry Ward was murdered by the IPLO as he tried to give them the slip from the Diamond Jubilee Bar in the Shankill. He got up to make a break for it when he saw the two gunmen walking in the door. They shot him five times with a 9mm pistol and a .38 revolver before fleeing. Although Harry was a UDA man he wasn't the target. The ASU had been looking for John 'Bunter' Graham, a UVF commander. Hours later taxi driver Hugh Magee was shot in retaliation.

Within weeks the attacks came closer to home when my lifelong friend Gerry Drumgoole was caught up in the crossfire. The two of us had even remained close when I was jailed for causing the death of his brother Maurice in a car crash. Gerry was a loyal UDA man and often hung out with me and some of the guys in C Company, but he wasn't an active gunman or involved in any paramilitary operations at all. Not that it made any difference.

On 13 November that year, the IRA launched a vicious assault, dubbed the Night of the Long Knives, on Protestant targets, leaving four people dead. UDA veteran Billy Kingsberry and his stepson, Sean Mehaffy, were shot dead in their home on Lecale Street. Two gunmen burst into their kitchen and opened fire with an AK-47 and a 9mm pistol. Kingsberry was holding his five-week-old grandchild when he was killed. Amazingly, the baby survived.

An hour later, brothers Stephen and Kenneth Lynn were gunned down in north Belfast. Neither of them had any paramilitary links, but it emerged that the bungalow they were renovating had recently been owned by a prominent

UVF member. The Provos had also smashed their way into a house owned by Joe Bratty, a leading man in the UDA in the south of the city. Luckily for him, he wasn't at home.

It was that same night that they went for Gerry. Both the Republicans and ourselves had someone whose sole job was to listen in to police scanners and pick up any information they could. Often important intelligence could be obtained in this way as information on what the RUC called 'players' was openly passed over the airwaves, including addresses and car registration details.

At the time both Gerry and I were driving the same type of car, a black Ford Orion Ghia. That night the IRA planted a bomb underneath his. I don't know if it was intended for me, but I suspect that it wasn't. It's possible they were hoping I was in the car when it went off, but I'm sure they would have known it was Gerry's and not mine. He lost part of one leg from the thigh down and also half of his arm in the explosion.

It was tough for Gerry, who not only went through months of rehabilitation but also found it hard to understand why the IRA had gone for him. Nor was it the last time he got caught up in sectarian conflict.

In September 1993, two INLA gunmen came looking for me on Hazelfield Street, where Gerry and I were now neighbours. The two hitmen walked into our street and spotted him having a cup of tea outside his front door. One of them was wearing mirror sunglasses and had his arm behind his back. Gerry was wise to what was going on and as he turned to go inside the rifles appeared. He managed to get himself partly behind the security door but one of the men walked up and shot him in the stomach. The other tried to make sure the job was finished by firing through the window. Moments later Gerry's wife and young daughter arrived home and came under fire before the INLA unit fled.

Within hours, C Company was out for revenge and planted a bomb at the home of Gino Gallagher, the leader of the INLA. He was so shaken by the explosion that the next day he appeared on television with his face blanked out, complaining that he was being targeted. Eventually he was shot dead as he signed on at the Falls Road Social Security office following an internal feud in January 1996.

Gerry survived both attempts on his life and in the end it was the UDA that forced him to leave the Shankill in 1995. A sledgehammer gang burst through his door and told him and his wife Jacqueline, who was the sister of informer Brian Nelson, to get out if they knew what was good for them. I was in prison at the time but still got the blame for his forced eviction. While I was behind bars I did everything I could for Gerry, and I knew nothing about what happened to him. Sadly, we have not spoken in years as a result. No matter what was going on while I was locked up, it was assumed that I'd given the go-ahead for it all.

Two months after the bombing of Gerry's car, an IRA landmine was placed underneath a van full of Protestant workers at Teebane crossroads. The explosion, on 17 January 1992, killed eight employees of the Ballymena firm Karl Construction. They were targeted by the IRA's East Tyrone brigade because they had been working at Lisanelly army base. The attack was a clear example of the difference between the Loyalist and Republican paramilitaries – the IRA selected targets that could for the most part be linked to the army or the RUC. I wanted to change our tactics so that we also went for 'legitimate' targets.

In retaliation for Teebane, a gun attack was launched on an Ormeau Road bookmaker's: two UFF gunmen walked in and opened fire with automatic rifles, killing five Catholics. The IRA had thought very carefully about who they were going to target in their killing campaigns in an attempt to give their actions some justification. Those eight men killed at Teebane had nothing to do with the paramilitaries but, because they had been building an army base, it was considered OK to blow them to bits.

To build support, I knew it was important that it was the real Republicans that were in the sights, unlike the bookmakers, if we were to gain the support of our own people and if we were going to put the Republicans under any pressure, or the Britsh army.

At the beginning of 1992, Belfast was on the verge of all-out war and the security services were desperate to get me behind bars. Despite the failure of Katherine Spruce's evidence to get the desired result, they were happy to believe another woman who fed them a line and thought my name was Johnny O'Dair. She told detectives that she turned up at UDA headquarters asking to speak to me as she had information that I would be interested in. She claimed we had sex in the car park of Belfast Zoo, and she also said that when I was dropping her off she pointed out the home of a taxi driver called Paddy Clarke. Two days after this allegedly happened, the 52-year-old was shot four times in his living room by a lone gunman.

On the strength of the woman's statement, I was held in Castlereagh, but released without charge after two days. C Company volunteer Sammy McKay was given seven years in September 1993 for helping get rid of a motorbike that had been used in the hit.

Two months later, Special Branch were after me, but this time it wasn't to lock me up. It was to get me on the payroll of Her Majesty's Government.

On 28 April that year, Philomena Hanna was shot dead just after she opened a pharmacy on Springfield Road. A gunman and his driver sped away on the back of a stolen motorcycle. The shop was close to Lanark Way, a route used all the time to cross the peace line by Loyalist and Republican ASUs. The UFF, claiming responsibility, said that she was a member of the IRA and was the sister of a Sinn Fein official, which her family denied. Along with James 'Sham' Millar and 'Baldy Dan' Fitzgerald, I was pulled in and questioned about Hanna's death.

The first two days in Castlereagh were tough. They gave me both barrels. Tables were slammed, the shouting was deafening and this time not a single cigarette was handed out. For the first 48 hours, I had no access to a solicitor, which was the norm. When he was allowed in, I told my brief that the coppers were going nowhere but I expected to be in for the full seven days. He said the other two had been released but confirmed that the police wanted to keep me locked up for as long as they could. I was surprised that they had released anyone. Normally they tried to make life as difficult as possible and kept us all banged up. If they had let Baldy Dan and Sham off the hook, clearly they had something else in mind for me.

First the screaming and the banging of the table stopped. I was sitting in the cell waiting for another barrage when two men walked in and introduced themselves as Special Branch officers. They told me that their boss wanted to pay me a personal visit, something that never happened as far as I knew. They were to pave the way for what was to come next. They started to rationalise the need for touts: 'You know, Johnny, there are informers at the top of the UDA and the IRA. Our job is to save lives and that is what we need information for.' It wasn't that they were trying to get convictions; no, it was about saving lives.

Then they started telling me how much they already knew, but not exactly what they knew. Information about me, places I'd been, people I'd been seen with. They weren't boasting that they had caught me in the act, just that they knew where I was and when I was there.

They told me I'd been to a small fishing village in County Down called Portavogie, where trawlers would make drops. But there was more to it than that. The spooks hadn't just been tipped off about it, they had been there in the background, watching. I rocked back on my chair in the cell and listened nervously as they related exactly what had happened.

When I'd been waiting, I'd started throwing fish to the seals in the harbour. One of the officers joked, 'Did you enjoy feeding the wildlife? Johnny, there are times when we are right next to you and you have no idea at all.'

The tactic was intended to freak me out, I reckoned. To let me know that they were keeping an eye on me, but not know how much they actually had on me. Then it was more of the same, and it got worse.

The taller of the two officers went on to recount a conversation I'd had outside a court after a hearing had been adjourned. I and a few other C Company men were deciding what cafe we were going to go to, and he knew what was said, word for word. So now I knew that they were watching me and had someone either feeding them conversations afterwards or wearing a wire.

The security for Gina and I was the next area they wanted to get me nervous about. On a good day, the two of us would drive up to Shawsbridge, on the outskirts of Belfast, and go for a bike ride to get a break from the city. It was supposed to be a secret, but they knew all about that as well. This time, his tone a bit more serious, the spook said, 'You're up there without a care in the world, not concerned about who else knows you're there, and we are right beside you.'

Then came the punchline. He asked me to work for them. Give them the details of operations before they happened. There would be a roadblock waiting, and lives would be saved. They were pulling all the strings. Even if I was on the job and was arrested, they promised my cover wouldn't be blown and everyone would be a winner. To seal the deal, the boss came into the cell after the groundwork had been done.

He was a tall guy, immaculately dressed, and carrying a briefcase. Rather than sit opposite me, he stood and placed the case between his legs. After checking that the two who had been in before him had been courteous, he got to the point and asked me what I thought of the offer. And I told him. There was no way I was going to be a tout and betray my organisation. But they knew that, so it was time for the suitcase. He laid it on the table and opened it.

Fifty-five thousand in new notes and another five £1,000 bundles of used notes. It was a lot of money and it was just the first instalment of my new wages. I was allowed to feel it in case I thought it was false – and I did. I'd never seen that much cash in my life.

There is an easy way to tell who can be turned: you look for the people who don't want to do time, or who like a bit of cash. Special Branch always started with these levers. They had nothing to lock me up for, and I wasn't ruled by cash. It got them nowhere, so back to my cell I went. But they weren't going to leave it at that.

Next thing, a woman was sent in to try to win me over. She was a good-looking girl wearing jeans and a jumper. I thought I knew her from the Shankill as well. She sat down beside me, offered me a cigarette and admitted she was also a Special Branch officer and had been on my case for a long, long time.

'Ah, Johnny,' she purred, 'what you're doing is madness. You're going to end up getting life sooner or later.' Then she dropped in, 'It's all about life and love. Fuck Special Branch! Fuck the UFF! I fancy you big time.'

They were desperate for me to fall for her, meet her on the outside and spill my guts.

As it got closer to the end of the week, they realised they had got nowhere with me. After the seven days, I was going to walk out, go back to the Shankill and carry on what I was doing. They had tried reasoning with me, putting cash on the table and then offering me sex. None of it worked. If anything, I'd learned more about them than they had about me.

When the time they could hold me expired, I was released without charge. But they had a surprise in store for me. A couple of days later, they raided a house and lifted a stolen army SA80 assault rifle. They had hoped that when I was released I would have explained to the others that the Branch agents had kept me in and tried to turn me. Next thing, a gun belonging to B Company is lifted off the streets and I look like a rat.

They had made a mistake. I had no idea where the gun was, and apparently it had been there for five years. It was all about slowly trying to break me down and make me agree to take their pieces of silver.

The same Special Branch team lifted me for another murder. The interviews started off on the same tack as before: how much did I want to come on board? But it didn't last. I was furious that they had tried to get me killed for being a rat and handing over guns. I told them where to stick the cash and that they would have more luck trying to shag their female colleague than getting me to be a tout. That didn't please them at all. The mood changed.

'Mr Adair, of course you're going to walk out of here a free man,' one of the coppers told me. 'But, see, when you get out it won't be as easy as you think. The IRA might not know too much about you now, but they will soon.'

He was right. At this stage, the IRA didn't really know who I was, much less had they tried to kill me. It was made clear to me that, since I wasn't going to play their game, the gloves were off and they were going to pull every trick in the book.

The first thing they were going to do was tell one of their Republican informers who I was, where I lived, what I looked like and what kind of car I drove. He was then to go back to his ASU and pass on the details, claiming that it had come from a source in the hospital from which personal details could be obtained to ensure that there was no suspicion placed on him. They were also going to tell the unit, through him, how to go about getting to me. There was no point trying to get through the front door as it was reinforced, and there was no point sticking a bomb under my car as I checked it. According to the Special Branch blueprint, the way to get me was to take over a house, or go to the places I had a habit of going to, such as the UDA headquarters or the school where I dropped off my kids.

They finished the threat by saying, 'Johnny, you go to whatever politician you want, Ian Paisley or whoever, and you tell them what we have spoken about. Who do you think they are going to believe? A murdering bastard like you, or respected police officers like us?'

And everything they said would happen did.

8

SETTLING SCORES

Just before 7am on 17 July 1992, two cars set off from the Loyalist Taughmonagh Estate for an address in the Andersonstown district of Belfast. It was the kind of intelligence that had to be acted on straight away.

A top Republican in Northern Ireland, Brian Gillen, and a couple of other senior Provos were due to hold a meeting at a house on Finachy Road. C Company's number-one team of Skelly, Jackie Thompson, Matt 'Muff' McCormick, Tommy Potts and Andy Watson were briefed and told what to do. The route was pretty straightforward apart from a bend in the road that had a blind spot at a railway bridge. That's where the security forces lay in wait.

Watson was in the lead car, which was clean and there to ferry the ASU to safety after the move had been made. Behind, Muff was at the wheel of the second car with Skelly alongside him and Thompson and Potts in the back. At Skelly's feet was the grip containing the fire-power: an AK-47, a Browning 9mm and a Sterling machine gun.

Having drifted ahead, Watson was over the brow of the hill before the murder car had reached the top. It was an ambush. Watson was already face down in the road by the time the second car could see what was waiting for them. A police car was parked sideways across the road with a marksman sprawled over the bonnet looking down the barrel of a gun and waiting to open up. There was no warning: he fired at the earliest opportunity.

In the front seat of Muff's car was a 14lb hammer that was to be used to smash the way into the property where the Republicans were meeting. It was all the excuse the security forces needed. They later claimed the hammer appeared to be a rifle and so had justified their firing at will. The truth was that they knew C Company's number-one team were about to walk into their trap.

The four men in the Opel threw themselves out as it was still moving and tried to run for it. Muff stumbled and was shot in the leg. Thompson was nabbed quickly, while Skelly and Potts were both rammed by police cars as they tried to escape. In the chaos an undercover army officer took a bullet from one of his own men. They were all hospitalised before they were taken to Castlereagh for questioning.

Local Republicans came out into the street to berate the cops, who they thought were lifting an IRA ASU. When they realised it was Loyalists who had been snared, they began shouting, 'Jail the bastards!'

A fatal mistake had been made in the planning of the hit: other members of the UDA were told what was going to happen and the team was sold down the river. If you were operating outside your own patch, it was normal to let the local brigadier know what was going down. In this case it was a Special Branch agent who tipped off his handlers. Nine months later, his handiwork got Skelly, Thompson and Potts 16 years, Muff 14 years and Watson ten years. Skelly had only been out of prison for 24 days when the operation failed. He had been caught hijacking a car for another operation but was given bail while he was waiting to go to court.

I was gutted. It was a massive blow to me personally and to C Company. These guys were my friends and they were crucial to the unit. With them off the streets, the security services were convinced C Company was drawing its final breath.

Far from it. An IRA bombing campaign made sure of that.

It started in September 1992 with a firebomb attack that wrecked the Hyde Park Hotel in London. Then it came closer to home. A 1,000lb bomb placed outside the Northern Ireland Forensic Laboratory on the Belvoir Estate in Belfast took out a thousand homes. A 200lb device exploded in Bangor. The same tactic was used again when the Provisionals left a car bomb outside a police station in the Protestant town of Glengormley and another hundred homes were badly damaged. It was all part of a Nationalist propaganda campaign to win support, especially in America.

Their targeting also gave them an air of legitimacy in the belief that the structures of the British state and all those who supported it were fair game.

On 6 November, a UFF statement warned that if there were more bombs in Protestant areas the 'Republican community as a whole' would face the consequences. It was ignored. A week later, a 500lb IRA car bomb devastated the Unionist town of Coleraine. Shops were wrecked and it was a miracle nobody was killed. The response was swift. The following afternoon two gunmen entered James Murray's betting shop on Oldpark Road and opened fire. Three men were left dead.

The previous month, Gerard O'Hara had been shot dead by two UFF gunmen at his home in North Queen Street. The family of the 18-year-old denied he had any links to Republican paramilitaries. It was through he was targeted in revenge for the murder of Scots Guardsman Damian Shackleton a few weeks earlier. The 24-year-old was riding in the back of an army Land Rover when he was shot in the chest.

C Company wasn't going to go away. Skelly and the best operators had been taken off the street, but there was no way that we were going to throw in the towel. Sections of the security forces realised this and it wasn't long before the warnings I'd received from the cops in Castlereagh became reality.

In March 1993, an IRA unit sat outside the UDA's head-quarters on Berlin Street watching my car and waiting for their moment. The Provos were top operators and knew their best chance of a kill would come once I'd climbed into the vehicle. I would be trapped with nowhere to go. If they pounced quickly enough, they could open up from point-blank range and it was very unlikely I would survive. Leading UFF gunmen went in and out of the building most of the day but they didn't flinch. It was me they wanted. The Shankill was packed with Saturday-afternoon shoppers but that wasn't going to stop them. My head of security, Donald Hodgen, was with me, as normal. Big Donald was alert all the time and was brilliant at sniffing out security forces and Republican gunmen.

The IRA team stuck to their plan and didn't get trigger-happy too early. They waited until we both got into my white Vauxhall Cavalier. Before we pulled away, Donald sensed something was wrong. About 100 yards away, on the other side of the road, was a bunch of guys in a car the same make and model as mine. Two were in the front and one was sitting in the middle of the two seats in the back. When I looked over, the driver of the car stared straight at me: no nerves, no sign of panic. The first thing I looked for was the telltale rolled-up balaclava or baseball cap, which could be pulled down to hide the face. He didn't have either on. I relaxed a bit. There was no fear in their eyes and they weren't making an effort to hide who they were.

Seconds later, Paul Orr, C Company's welfare officer, who had been with me when we left the UDA building, climbed into his car and parked behind the IRA unit's motor. Nothing happened to him, so I was sure that there was no threat. I glanced down to put the key in the ignition. Before

I could look up again to pull away, Donald was screaming my name. Next came the flashes from the barrel of the AK-47 as the gunman ran towards the car firing at me. The first burst of rounds came through the window. I slumped towards the middle of the car to try to get some protection. Donald was gone: he had managed to get out of the passenger side, but took a bullet in the leg as he ran for cover.

As I crouched down in the car, the gunman kept firing. I could hear the high-pitched noise of the bullets slicing through the bodywork, and the dull crash as they slammed into the engine. Then all I could feel was a scorching pain in my side. I knew I'd been hit. I closed my eyes and grabbed where the pain was coming from. I thought my insides were about to fall through the wound. I waited for the bullet to hit me in the head. There was nowhere to go. The headrest had been shot to bits and the car was riddled with holes. Then the gunshots stopped, followed by the roar of the getaway car as it raced off.

As the IRA team left the scene, one of them hung out the window, brandishing the AK-47, and shouted, 'Where the fuck is your Johnny Adair now?'

They were sure they had killed me. When I slumped over in the driver's seat they assumed the life was seeping out of me.

I got myself out of the car and staggered up the road. People had appeared from everywhere to see what was going on. I was still gripping my side, scared to look at the damage. A UFF guy came up to me and pulled my hand away before ripping open my shirt and telling me I was all right. The bullet had just grazed me.

SETTLING SCORES

The IRA dumped the car outside bookmaker Sean Graham's place on the Ormeau Road, which had been targeted following the Teebane atrocity. They were blaming me for what had happened and this was a message to Loyalists. The words of the Special Branch officers who tried to recruit me were ringing in my ears. This was them getting their own back. I'm not saying the IRA knew they were doing the Branch's dirty work, but that was where the intelligence was coming from.

One man was to be sent down for the attempt on my life. Stephen Larkin, a former French Foreign Legionnaire, was given 16 years in March 1993. When it was first announced on the news that he had been charged, a Loyalist team found out where he lived and shot anything that moved at the address. As it turned out, there was nobody there but his dog – and the dog got it.

Three years later, Larkin was freed after a witness told the court at his retrial that Larkin had been drinking in the Highfield Club in the Ardoyne at the time he was supposed to have been taking pot-shots at me. The witness claimed he had been too frightened at the original trial to come forward.

The order for my killing had been issued by the IRA's commander in north Belfast, who was furious when he realised I was still alive. There was no way he was going to accept the failure and he wanted it sorted straight away. I would have done the same thing myself. A copper once said to me in Castlereagh that the only difference between the IRA commander and me was the flag we fought for. He was right.

On the night of the Berlin Street attack, he would have been sitting down waiting for the television news to come on so he could admire his handiwork. Imagine his reaction when he found out that I was only slightly injured. Someone was going to pay and it was my associate Norman Truesdale.

Days later, two gunmen burst into Norman's sweet shop on the corner of Oldpark Road and Century Street and shot him as he was serving a 12-year-old boy. The first figure, who was wearing a balaclava, shot him in the chest with a handgun from close range. As he lay on the ground, the second gunman followed up with a burst of fire from an AK. The whole attack was caught on film by a hidden security camera, and a guy called Thomas McWilliams from the Ardoyne later admitted the murder. As he was led from the dock, the guilty man shouted, 'Up the IRA!'

An IRA man later also admitted that he held a family hostage and hijacked their car in the Oldpark area. He then told detectives how an ASU used the motor to travel to my kids' school, where they planned to murder me as I dropped them off. Luckily, I didn't turn up and they returned the car to the family, telling them not to report the incident to the RUC.

The second of Norman's killers has never been convicted. The Truesdale family were members of the UDA but Norman was never a member of a sectarian murder gang, as the IRA's newspaper *An Phoblacht* had claimed. He was targeted because he hadn't handed over cash. He had a fruit machine in his shop and it was an accepted fact of life that paramilitaries took a slice of the money that was put in and handed it over to prisoners. Because he wouldn't pay, they took away the machine.

The guy who was supposed to collect money from Norman also took it from machines in the Ardoyne. He told the IRA that Norman was providing funds for the UDA, effectively issuing his death warrant. The IRA showed their hand in a statement issued afterwards which said that Norman had been killed for his involvement in extortion.

Years later, when I was locked up, a Republican prisoner told me that the person who had carried out the hit had only ever done that one personally. Norman wasn't the only person to be killed in the shop. IPLO gunmen drew up in a car in September 1988 and shot the previous owner in the head. He was Billy Quee, a well-known UDA man with five kids, and it is thought Martin 'Rook' O'Prey was behind the hit.

On 20 March 1993, an IRA cell on the mainland struck, this time in Warrington. A month earlier, an explosion at a gasworks there had caused a huge fireball but nobody was injured. This time two devices went off in the town's busy shopping precinct, killing a three-year-old and a twelve-year-old. An investigation later discovered that the bombs had been left in cast-iron bins to create large amounts of shrapnel.

After Warrington, there was a massive public backlash against the Republicans, just as there had been after the Enniskillen Remembrance Day explosion in 1987. In Dublin, thousands took to the streets to protest.

The following month, another bomb went off, this time in central London, killing a newspaper photographer and injuring more than 40 other people. The device had been left in a van parked in Bishopsgate. Police had received a coded warning and were evacuating the area when the bomb went off.

The IRA were behind the attacks, both on the mainland and in Northern Ireland. Anyone connected to the IRA or their political wing Sinn Fein were fair game. There was no way we were going to sit back and watch what they were doing. But it wouldn't be easy. All of them lived in staunchly Nationalist areas and most of their homes had a full range of security measures in place.

On 24 March, a grenade was lobbed through the upstairs window of councillor Gerard McGuigan's home in the Ardoyne. Nobody was killed but a massive hole was blasted in the bedroom floor. The house had been watched and the security was tight, so there was little chance of entry through the front door or the windows. But that hadn't meant nothing could be done. The following day, a carbon copy of the attack was launched at the home of Sinn Fein councillor Joe Austin.

Hours after the attack on McGuigan's home, Sinn Fein activist Peter Gallagher was shot dead after arriving at work near Distillery Street in west Belfast. The gunman had a 9mm Browning which he fired from bushes, hitting his target ten times before making his escape on a bicycle along the nearby Westlink.

The following day, at Castlerock in County Londonderry,

the UFF's north Antrim brigade killed four Catholic workmen who were carrying out renovation. Among the dead was the IRA's OC in the area, James Kelly. That same night, a teenage Catholic named Damien Walsh was shot dead by the UFF as he worked on a youth training scheme near Twinbrook. This was the reality of what was going on: tit-for-tat attacks all over the Province.

On 1 May 1993, a C Company team was sent to Sinn Fein councillor Alex Maskey's house on Gartree Place in Andersonstown. The unit opened fire as they arrived, then chased Maskey's friend Alan Lundy into the house, where he was helping build a porch to provide extra security. Maskey escaped unhurt by hiding in the bathroom. Lundy, who was killed, had been jailed for ten years in 1972 after being caught planting a bomb in the Shakespeare Bar in Belfast.

But things didn't always go to plan. Two C Company volunteers, James and Rab Hill, were sent to carry out an assault on a Sinn Fein advice centre in the city's New Lodge area. The chances of getting through the door were slim but reconnaissance revealed the glass in the kitchen wasn't bulletproof, so that was the weakness the two-man team would have to exploit. If they managed to unload enough rounds, their chances of hitting someone were very high.

The Hill brothers drove into the area without trouble. After stopping outside the target, one of them quickly made his way to the window and emptied the AK-47's magazine through it. The next step was to get to the safety of the nearby peace line at Tigers Bay. But then the plan started to unravel. Adjacent to the advice centre was a high-rise block of flats and on top of it was an army observation post. As they made their getaway, James was hit in the back by a round from an SA80. There was blood everywhere. Rab gathered him up as best he could and made for a gate leading out of the Republican area, where another car should have been waiting.

But the driver had panicked when he heard the army sharpshooter open fire and had disappeared. Rab now had to get to the safe house on Copperfield Street with a smoking AK-47 on one arm and his dying brother on the other. He knew he couldn't do both, so he made a snap decision. James was left in an alley in the hope that the paramedics would get to him in time and Rab made for the safe house to get cleaned up.

In minutes, the cops were all over the place and soon tracked Rab down by a trail of blood that led to the front door. A specialist RUC team was brought in to surround the house as they thought there might be hostages inside. Eventually, they stormed it and dragged Rab out in his underwear. Jamie survived and the brothers were sentenced to 16 years in jail.

Not long after the incident, I was passed a message from a soldier who wanted to apologise for what had happened. He thought the Hills were an IRA unit.

We lagged behind the IRA in terms of explosives. They had both the monopoly on the supply of Semtex and skill in its use. But C Company wasn't without ability and developed a brick bomb to target a Sinn Fein councillor.

SETTLING SCORES

During the 1990s, Republican Belfast was rife with joyriders who were breaking into cars every night. The plan was to break the side window of the councillor's car, steal the stereo and leave the brick bomb on the seat. As soon as the brick was lifted it would detonate. It was a devious bit of kit, but on this occasion the councillor was suspicious and called in the cops to make the bomb safe.

Booby-trapped chocolate boxes also became a popular weapon and were often left on the doorsteps of Republican sympathisers.

There were no limits to the struggle. Some people would think it wrong to target women and that's understandable. But C Company did it. On 27 July 1993, a unit was sent to Twinbrook to the home of Sinn Fein councillor Annie Armstrong. To us, being a part of Gerry Adams's party was as good as being in the IRA.

The two-man team drove to the house, aiming to con her into coming out from behind the protection of the steel-reinforced front door and into the gunman's sights. But when Armstrong heard his voice through the intercom she knew something was wrong. The gunman, hearing panic in her reply, immediately blasted as many rounds as he could into the house. As in some other attacks, there were no casualties, but C Company was now being taken seriously. Republicans weren't as safe as they thought as they lay in bed at night, even those whose involvement was in the past.

In 1980, Edward Brophy had been acquitted, after an 11-week trial, of involvement in one of the worst atrocities of the Troubles: the La Mon House bombing. Two years earlier, an incendiary device had been planted at the restaurant, on the outskirts of Belfast, which killed 12 Protestants attending the Irish Collie Club annual dinner. The IRA had given a nine-minute warning. It was the day before Gerry Adams was arrested and charged with membership of the IRA, an accusation that he has always denied. The case never came to court.

Brophy had been cleared of the attack when the judge ruled that his alleged confessions were inadmissible, but he was given five years for membership of the IRA.

When C Company received intelligence that Brophy was working in a clothes shop in the docks area of Belfast in the 1990s, revenge for the attack was the only thought. The shop was put under continuous surveillance, the inside was checked out and he was spotted working behind the counter on a number of occasions. A two-man team was sent to carry out the mission, a driver and a gunman. Brophy was shot several times from point-blank range and the ASU made their getaway. He survived.

9

BETRAYAL

The security services in Northern Ireland, particularly Special Branch, hated me. As C Company carried out more and more operations the pressure to get me off the street was close to suffocating them. All their sources of information, no matter how trivial, were being grabbed with both hands and squeezed for every drop of intelligence.

I wasn't well educated but I was streetwise. I knew that if I was going to keep one step ahead I had to learn from them so as to make myself stronger. Even the copper who claims responsibility for eventually jailing me, Jonty Brown, admitted I ran rings round them. It sickened the officers.

Whenever Special Branch discovered someone who had links to me, that person was subjected to non-stop harassment and pushed to the edge to come up with the goods on me. The obvious people, like my neighbour, were the first to be targeted, and the approach was by no means casual. To make sure they knew what buttons to press, the Branch's agents went through that person's life in minute detail and calculated the most vulnerable areas, the tender spots that, when prodded, would make them dance to their tune.

My neighbour was a taxi driver and he was pulled over by the police at 2am. The excuse was that he had gone through a red light. Instead of dealing with it at the side of the road, the officers hauled him back to the police station. Once he was in the interview room, it became clear to him why the heavy-handed tactics were being rolled out. If he had run a red light, which was by no means certain, it was a set-up to get to me.

The Branch money team had pulled apart the man's finances and spotted a weakness. Now, unless he took details of every car that came and went from my house – make, model and registration number, as well as times and who was in the vehicles – his plan to buy a new house would be in tatters. He was saving up to buy a new place and was doing two jobs. The cash he brought in as a cabbie was essential to secure the mortgage. All that would stop if he lost his licence – not hard to arrange for Special Branch. Inform on your neighbour or we will shatter your dreams. Thankfully, he was one of the few who told me they had been approached.

Most of the time, the formula was very similar. Pull in a volunteer that they had something on, tell him he was in line for a long stretch behind bars, then dangle the carrot of a 'Get out of jail free' card in front of them.

Belfast was always a tough place to move about, but especially so when Special Branch were after you. I was stopped and searched every time I was on the road. As a result, couriers were brought on board who were able to move around with more freedom.

One of our runners was a UDR man who had an army pass, which meant it was easier for him to navigate roadblocks. The RUC were much less likely to pull his car to bits. However, his identity and what he was up to were leaked to the Branch. He was on his way to work at 7am when a police Land Rover forced him to the side of the road and he was told to get out. Thinking there was no reason for them to be suspicious, he did what he was told. As he strode towards the back of the Land Rover, the doors sprang open.

A copper walking behind him barked, 'Get fucking in there!'

Sitting in the back was a plain-clothes officer with a suitcase between his legs. The doors banged shut behind him and the seated man, who identified himself as Shane, spoke. 'I have an insurance policy for you, and it's in this suitcase. Adair won't think twice about putting two in your head and leaving you in a hole in the ground. He's a bastard and a scumbag. We know that you haven't killed anybody, but we do know what you're doing. Go away and think about this, and we'll get back to you.'

Again, I was informed about the approach. The pressure of being a tout wasn't worth living with and the guy came and told me what had happened. Rather than sitting and waiting for their dirty tricks to start, we decided it was worth trying to play them at their own game.

The agent was to be contacted on a phone number which was handed over in the back of the Land Rover. Pretending to be their target, I gave the spook a call to see what he had to say for himself and what they had up their sleeve. The scam didn't last long as he figured out he was talking to me.

I told him the conversation had been recorded and his threats of terrible consequences if the target didn't come on board were now on record. He was horrified, although in fact I hadn't recorded it at all. Teams of cops smashed through dozens of doors trying to find the non-existent tape. It was just another part of the war between us, but it kept them off my back for a while. I had to show them they weren't getting to me and that the people around me weren't going to sell me down the river.

On more than one occasion, their attempts at harassment blew up in their faces. It was impossible for me to move about the city without getting pulled up by the security forces for a spot check. Anything they could do to disrupt me and give me aggro, they did. They would even wind me up about my two handicapped sisters. One cop in particular told me he had something urgent to tell me about 'a sister', and, when I asked which one, he taunted, 'The simple one.'

The patrols would often make me open the bonnet of my car and they particularly enjoyed pulling out a fuse to leave me stranded at the side of the road as they drove off. It stopped, though, after one squad car did it and later that day thought it would be a good idea to drive past my house. As they turned round in the cul de sac to head off, after waving at me to remind me what had happened, two gunmen jumped out and opened fire on the vehicle. It was an armoured car, but a bullet ricocheted off the ground and embedded itself in a passenger's leg. Not long afterwards a piece of graffiti appeared on a wall: 'RUC kneecapped for anti-social behaviour – stealing Johnny's fuse.'

To try to protect me and the rest of C Company from Special Branch's tactics, an effort was made to recruit people that the Branch knew nothing about at all. One of these was a character named Tommy Beggs, a tailor by day who knew how to keep himself in the clear. When Beggs became active, he wanted nothing to do with the rest of the C Company crowd and promised that he wouldn't come to my house. All he asked for was to be given instructions, and he'd do it. The only catch was, it had to be first thing in the morning or last thing at night, to leave him free to go to work. It was a perfect situation for the C Company. Beggs wasn't going to be hanging about with any of the other players in the unit and there was nothing about him that was going to flag him up to the cops.

To keep him off the RUC's radar, whenever he was available to help C Company met his military commander away from the Shankill. Beggs was never a gunman, only ever the driver, and that made the relationship easier. Before anything happened, he would be given the address that was being targeted so that he could familiarise himself with the area. On the day of the operation, he would be told what time he had to be at the safe house to pick up the team. He would wear his shirt and tie under his boiler suit to collect the unit – we called him the 'Shirt and Tie Man' – take them to their destination and then give them a lift back to the second safe house. He would take the car to be ditched, take off his boiler suit and go to work. There would be no contact with him until another job was on.

I had a lot of admiration for Beggs for being so cool and able to live a double life. He allowed us to move around the city and that was essential. My movements were being constantly checked to see if there was any sort of pattern. If I was spotted outside an address which was later targeted, this was enough excuse for them to haul me in. The key for me was to keep things as random and sporadic as possible. Beggs didn't have that problem. He was off the radar.

The fight with the security forces was as intensive as taking on the Republican paramilitaries, to the point where teenage kids that I hardly knew were pulled in and squeezed. There was one local lad who did the odd bit of work; nothing serious, just a bit of running about. Intelligence officers knew, though, that even the most insignificant information could help them. One day the kid was arrested for shoplifting and taken to the police station. Ordinarily a quick caution would have been dished out and he would have been sent on his way. But, just when he thought he was about to be kicked out into the street, the RUC cop told him there were another couple of officers who wanted a chat with him.

First, they slapped down a picture of me and demanded

to know what the kid knew. He might have had a few run-ins with the police before but this was different. The pressure was cranked up a few notches, fists were slammed down on the table, there was screaming and shouting and he was warned what would happen if he didn't play ball.

The first thing the kid did was come to me and let me know the Branch were leaning on him. There was no way I was going to let them send a kid to spy on me, so the two of us went back to the police station. I got to the desk and told the inspector to go and get the Branch lads. If they wanted to ask me something, here I was. They should have the bottle to speak to me face to face and not send a 16-year-old to do their dirty work for them.

Then there were those who never told me. Throughout the history of C Company, there were touts who would take the cash for tip-offs and have their mates locked up.

When I was on remand waiting for the Katherine Spruce charges to be heard in court, Ken Barrett took over my role as military commander of C Company and all operations came to a halt. During that time, the UDA Inner Council discovered a Special Branch mole called Glenn Greer who was feeding vital information back to his handlers. He coughed to the lot: where, when and how he was recruited, how much money he was getting paid and what details he had passed on to the Branch.

Normally when someone confesses to passing on UDA secrets the sentence is death. But on this occasion Barrett, along with UDA top brass including Alec Kerr, gave him money and told him to disappear to Scotland.

For a while, Greer kept his head down, but he made the mistake of coming back to Northern Ireland. In October 1997, members of C Company tracked him down to his home on Bangor's Kilcooley Estate. A booby-trap made of two pounds of Powergel was placed underneath his Vauxhall Cavalier and exploded within yards of the house. He was inside the car and died.

The Greer case made it clear that there were few, if any, at the top of the UDA who could be trusted. Even when the leadership were told what had been going on, nothing was done. They were asked for permission for Barrett to be punished but it was refused. Clearly, Special Branch's influence went right to the top of the UDA.

Billy Stobie was the UDA's quartermaster, and suspicions were first raised about him when he walked away from firearms charges in 1990. During the trial, he asked his solicitor to tell the Crown's lawyer privately that he would reveal all about the Finucane case if he was convicted. Moments later, a policeman referred to previous convictions and the case was thrown out. We had no idea that he threatened to tell all but he walked free from court and it all seemed too good to be true. Things went quiet for a while. He was with A Company at the top of the Shankill, so it wasn't really our problem.

When Stobie got a job with a taxi firm called Circle Cabs, it all changed. The firm was controlled by C Company and was nicknamed 'Murder Cabs' by the police because the cars were always being hijacked and used in operations. Special Branch wanted eyes and ears on the ground, people who knew what was going on, so they recruited the likes of bar staff and taxi drivers. With Circle Cabs being used in so many operations, they decided that Stobie, who was running the desk, was going to help them again. But he slipped up.

A taxi was hijacked for an operation which was pulled at the last minute. The motor was returned to the owner, who was instructed not to report it to the RUC. The next day, the cops started asking questions and one of the team was arrested. Straight away fingers were pointed at Stobie, as everyone else involved was watertight. Other things had been happening at the cab depot since he appeared on the scene that didn't add up. It was clear he was up to something and it wasn't going to be allowed to stand. Unlike with Greer, nobody was going to be asked for permission.

On 21 May 1992, Stobie was summoned to a house on Snugville Street where a party was going on to celebrate the release of Jackie Thompson on bail. He had been locked up after cops found radio scanners in his house. Stobie was shot five times in the back as he tried to run for it when he realised the pressure was on to explain what had happened. He lived.

When the others learned what had gone on, they were furious. In an effort to throw people off the scent, they even put a story out that Stobie had been dealt with because he was caught sleeping with a prisoner's wife. But in the end the suspicions about Stobie were proved to be correct. The extent of his involvement with Special Branch was exposed during the police investigation into Pat Finucane's murder.

On 12 December 2001, Stobie was shot as he prepared to take his girlfriend Lorraine Graham to work. The gunman hit him three times. Later that day, the Red Hand Defenders claimed responsibility and said his execution was for 'crimes against Loyalism'.

Two weeks before his death, Stobie walked free from court, where he was facing trial for allegedly being involved in the killing of Finucane. The court heard how he had been an agent from 1987 to 1990, and he admitted providing the weapons used in the hit but insisted he didn't know the target. Stobie also claimed he tipped off the security services both while the murder was in the planning stage and on the day it occurred. The case collapsed when it was ruled that a key witness couldn't give evidence owing to his fragile mental state. What sealed Stobie's fate, however, was what he said outside, on the steps of the court. He insisted the Finucane family deserved a 'proper inquiry' and, with his case over, the investigation should happen immediately.

Despite the pressure, he and his girlfriend decided to stay in Belfast. After his call for full disclosure and investigation into the Finucane murder, this wasn't a good idea. Stobie provided the guns for the hit and knew too much. There were a lot of nervous people. If more intelligence files were going to be opened, there was a real risk that the truth about the killing would be exposed. Key people knew their time was running out and ordered Stobie to be killed. Stobie had been told that there was no problem with his staying in Northern Ireland, but the minute he called for a full investigation into the Finucane case his fate was sealed.

While Stobie provided the Branch with a massive amount of intelligence, their biggest coup was flipping Mac. For a while he had been my right-hand man, a senior member of C Company and a very close friend. His betrayal was as tough to take as losing Skelly and the rest of the ASU on the operation in 1992.

Before he got heavily involved in C Company, Mac had been done for an attempted murder in the 1980s which I knew nothing about. He gave the cops a statement admitting what he had done but, rather than face prosecution, he accepted the offer of a deal. He would feed back information to them and in return the attempted murder would be discreetly forgotten.

The flow of information started slowly. When his handlers needed to look good, he would tell them where a stash of weapons could be found. That was fine for a while and for the most part he managed to keep them off his back. But the rules changed when they realised how high up in C Company Mac was going and that he had a good relationship with me. It was an opportunity the spooks weren't going to let slip through their fingers. The time had come to put him under a bit more pressure to come up with the goods.

It began after he was arrested for stealing a roof rack after a night's drinking. He was released on bail but he got the jitters and refused to go to court. Mac knew if he turned up to face the charges the Branch would be all over him. He wasn't going to give them the chance and even refused to collect any social security money. Mac was petrified because he knew they were going to start turning the screw to get to him. He was right to be.

At first it was gentle, just letting him know they were on his case. The first incident came when he was walking through town with some C Company heavies. Out of nowhere, a guy deliberately stuck his shoulder into him as he walked past. The normal reaction would have been to get hold of the culprit and teach him some manners. Nothing happened because as Mac turned to have a go he realised the guy was his Branch handler.

About half an hour later, Mac and the lads were eating in a cafe when the same bloke came up to the table and asked if he could borrow the salt. When he leaned over to pick it up off the table, he looked straight into Mac's eyes and held his gaze. The unspoken message was, 'You're not getting away from us that easily. We're on to you.'

Mac had the potential to be their best asset among Loyalist paramilitaries. C Company was the most active and he was right at the centre of what was going on. They weren't going to let him off the hook. Not long after the cafe incident, he got a knock at his front door. When his wife answered, two RUC officers in uniform asked if they could speak with Mac.

It was dark and because their hats were slightly pulled down he couldn't make out their faces as he strode to the door. From out of the gloom, one of them stepped forward into the light and raised his hat. It was his handler, who said sternly, 'Mac, it's a dirty war, and you're part of that dirty war. There's no way out of it,' before turning and leaving.

C Company had Special Branch rattled and they were desperate to get me off the streets. Mac was the man for the job and the plan was to set me up. I would be in a car with him in a Nationalist area where the cops would have a roadblock waiting at a prearranged spot. During the search Mac would be allowed to escape, but they would be sure to get me and a planted C Company gun that had a bit of history. As simple as that. They sold it to him, insisting that he was doing the right thing and was 'the man that can stop all of this'.

But Mac had a problem. The agents were desperate to know about operations in advance to allow arrests and protect targets. The way we operated, it wasn't as straightforward as that. Often a cell would be driving in no particular direction and the word was given to go. It couldn't be predicted.

Mac offered his handler more stashes of guns, but they weren't interested in that. It was rock-solid inside stuff they wanted. The more pressure they put on him, the more risks he began to take.

I first got suspicious about Mac when he left a weapon behind on an operation to target prominent members of the IPLO. Two names were passed to members of the UDA while they were being held at Castlereagh as being responsible for the murder of Protestants Thomas Gorman and Barry Watson. Both men were drinking in the Donegall Arms just before Christmas 1991 when the IPLO burst into the bar and opened fire with a revolver and a sawn-off shotgun. The targets lived in south Belfast but the UDA there asked C Company to step in and take over the retaliation.

Surveillance of one target's house had revealed that he not only had the usual reinforced doors, but also what looked like prison bars over his windows on both floors. No way was anyone getting into that house. But, despite the hyper-cautious security, a five-man team armed with handguns was dispatched to send him a message. A grenade was lobbed at the property and the house raked with gunfire.

The other address was also a dead-end. When the sledgehammer team smashed through the first door, they discovered a grille on the inside, but they made sure that he knew C Company had been there. While the team was making its exit from the area, Mac announced he had dropped a weapon. Alarm bells started to ring. If the Branch couldn't be told in advance of an operation going down, the least their tout could do was leave them something at the scene of the hit. I know for a fact that he stopped one hit. Sinn Fein councillor Alex Maskey was let off the hook. Mac was lying in wait for him as he came out of Crumlin Road Court and made his way to his car. He was ten feet away from him but the trigger wasn't squeezed. Mac claimed there was a police Jeep in the area, but it was nonsense. There was someone in the area watching what was going on. Mac had him at his mercy, but let him go.

Mac was close to breaking and was reduced to giving them anything he could. It got to the stage where he was telling them a street where he had dropped me off in the hope that I'd stashed a weapon there or there was something else they could pin on me. In the space of a week, they smashed down the doors of 11 addresses. All they turned up was a few rounds of ammunition. His handlers were going nuts. He wasn't delivering the goods, yet as far as they knew he was my right-hand man.

The police were so frustrated that they showed their hand in desperation. On the strength of Mac's information, a raid was carried out at Gerry Drumgoole's. The house was pulled apart as they looked for a scanner which let us listen in to the cops.

They drew a blank, but hours later they were back.

When the RUC informed Special Branch that the first search turned up nothing, they leaned on Mac. On the second visit, they were armed with more accurate information. The scanner was in an arm of Gerry's sofa. I turned up at the scene as the second search was being carried out. I tried to force my way into the house but the cops turned me away from the door. They could see I was upset about what was going on. One officer was told to follow me and keep eyes on me all the time. The rest of them got back into their Jeeps, concerned that something was going to happen.

I went to my house and took a bottle of milk out of the fridge. I stood right in front of the window where the cop could see me. He was doing his best to wind me up when an explosion rocked the street. My windows were blown in and he took the brunt of the blast. By the time the situation calmed down and the officer had been taken to hospital, there was a full-blown argument in the street between my men and the RUC. We were furious about the level of harassment and the number of raids being carried out. Then they let it slip.

'It's nothing to do with me,' the officer pleaded. 'It's your right-hand man who's making this happen.'

Mac wasn't there at the time and it was clear to all of us that he was the tout.

He knew his number was up and the pressure had got to him. He bolted. Despite what had happened, I was desperate to get in touch with him. I knew he was still in contact with his family, so I got them to arrange a meet. I wanted to know what the Branch were up to and eventually he agreed. The location was Newtownards. When I got there, I walked right past him as he looked like a tramp, doubled up with a heavy beard. Once I'd convinced him I was alone and unarmed, the two of us went to a cafe, where I bought him a burger and chips and a Coke. But he wouldn't touch any of it as he was paranoid that I might poison him. I tried to persuade him everything was OK and I wanted him back on board. The security services piled on the pressure and to keep them off his back he had given them a few weapons. It was no big deal. But he came round a bit and agreed to give me the 'name' of his handler and how he contacted him.

Back in Belfast, I decided to have another go at playing them at their own game. I called the number and then gave the name 'Glen Bank'. I was put through to the agent. He was delighted: his number-one asset was back on board. To secure the relationship, a 'big drop' was on the table, meaning the latest instalment of Mac's cash was going to be handed over.

There was a problem. It was to happen at 'the usual place' but I had no idea where that was. I tried to bluff and insist on a new location because I was being watched by C Company heavies. He wouldn't bite and was getting suspicious. The only deal on the table was that he would see what he could do and call me back. The trouble was, that call would be to Mac's house and he had disappeared. We got into the house and waited for the call but it never came. Either they got suspicious about the change in routine, or Mac got in touch with them to warn them off. I tried to phone the handler's number but it was out of service. What happened with Mac was a real shame. I trusted him a lot. Enough to bring him in from the cold. But he thought it was a trap. The last I heard of him, he had been moved to the mainland.

The wheels came off for Mac because he thought he could handle them but they weren't interested in the odd gun. The spooks needed to know the next operation inside out. Where was it going to happen? Who was the target? And when?

10

FACE TO FACE

The Shankill bomb was intended for me. If the IRA got any other members of the UDA, it was a bonus. Any civilian casualties would just have to be accepted. They were in the wrong place at the wrong time as far as the Provos were concerned. It was a massive gamble on shoddy intelligence and everybody lost. Even if the IRA are to be believed – that it wasn't a naked sectarian attack – the fact is the device was planted on a busy high street on a Saturday afternoon. Two months before the explosion that killed nine innocent Protestants, I came face to face with one of the bombers.

Gina and I were making our way home from a trip to the shops with the kids when we stopped at a set of lights at Carlisle Circus. Seconds later, a car packed with five men came to a halt next to us. In the back was the IRA's main man in north Belfast and among the other passengers was a young guy with bright-ginger hair and massive ears. Within seconds, the windows were down and a shouting match started. The IRA man was the only face I knew in their motor but he was saying little. It was the youngster in the front who was giving it all he had. Throughout the volley of abuse, he kept his hand up to his face with his fingers spread as wide as possible to hide his identity. Only when the lights turned green and he spat at me did I get a better look at him. I didn't think anything of it and assumed he wanted to make sure I didn't know who he was.

The IRA man went bleating to Oldpark police station straight away to make a complaint that I'd threatened to kill him when we were at the lights. Later that night, a C Company unit went to his sister's place, which he was using as a safe house, and tried to force their way in. When it became clear it wasn't going to happen, the building was peppered with gunfire.

At the rear of the address, the IRA men did a runner down an alley, straight into an army foot patrol. The soldiers thought they were under attack. When the senior IRA man came complaining for the second time in the night that he was being targeted, they fell about laughing.

His ginger sidekick was Thomas Begley, who on 23 October 1993 strolled into Fizzell's fish shop and blew himself up when the device went off early. On the morning of the bomb, I walked into 275a Shankill Road, above the fish shop, to collect a visitor's pass for the Maze. I was there no more than a couple of minutes before heading to see

Skelly in prison. After the visit, I went to the Donegall Arms and that is where I first heard what had happened. All I got was half a story. A bomb had gone off on the Shankill and people were injured. That was it. It was horrific when we got there.

There was black smoke everywhere and the noise of car alarms filled the air. Police officers and paramedics were swarming all over the place trying to do what they could for those who were hurt. The entire UDA building was floored. All that remained was rubble which spilled out across the road. I stood and watched as the bodies of women and children were being pulled out. In all, 57 people were injured. Two children, aged seven and 13, along with four women, were among the nine Protestants killed.

Bombers Thomas Begley and Sean Kelly were wearing white coats to give the impression they were delivery men when they made their way to the shop. The pair of them had dumped their car on Berlin Street, 500 yards from Fizzell's. Two months earlier at Carlisle Circus, Begley had known the plan. He worried then that if he showed his face there was a chance he could get spotted carrying the bomb to the fish shop.

When the IRA admitted responsibility, they claimed that I was the intended target and a UDA Inner Council meeting was scheduled for that morning. Lies. The offices were open six days a week and on a Saturday it was either for collecting visit cards or making loan payments. It was a long time since the building had been used for any Inner Council meeting. Their intelligence, if they even had any, was totally wrong. For many, it was a throwback to 20 years earlier, when IRA bombers had gone out and killed as many people as possible. It was a sectarian act and nothing else.

Kelly received nine life sentences in January 1995 and was told by the judge, 'This wanton slaughter of so many innocent people must rank as one of the most outrageous atrocities endured by the people of the province in the last quarter of a century.'

In 1998, he was given ten days' Christmas parole and at the end of July 2000 he was released under the Good Friday Agreement. Gerry Adams helped carry Thomas Begley's coffin at his funeral. Begley was also blamed by the widow of Stephen Waller, a member of the Royal Irish Regiment, for his murder while on Christmas leave the year before.

Something had to be done and the UDA held a meeting as quickly as possible after the attack. The Inner Council, of which I was a member, was questioned about how we would retaliate. Everyone was making the right noises, saying they were going to do this and do that. The gloves were off and nothing was off limits. A message had to be sent back to the IRA and the Catholic community who were supporting them. The official statement was: 'John Hume, Gerry Adams and the Nationalist electorate will pay a heavy, heavy price for today's atrocity. There will be no hiding place. Time is on our side.'

However, there were Special Branch informers at the meeting that night and I'm glad there were. One of the plans was to target a chapel in north Belfast. A UFF team were going to open fire at will. The team, a car and weapons were all put in place. A dummy run was also carried out. Thankfully, word of the plan had been leaked to Special Branch and the Catholic worshippers had been warned to stay away. It would have been truly dreadful if something like that had gone ahead.

Within hours of the bomb, Freddie Douglas, Peter Gilliland and another man travelled to the Boundary Bar in the Bawnmore district of Belfast and carried out a revenge attack by shooting a man in the arm. On the way back from the shooting, they drove too fast and were stopped by the traffic police. Douglas and Gilliland were jailed for the shooting; the third man escaped.

The next act of revenge came on 26 October when two Catholic bin men were killed and five others injured at the cleansing department on Kennedy Way. C Company man Tommy Beggs was sentenced to 144 years for his role in the attack. A UFF team travelled to the bin yard and opened fire, and it was Beggs who drove the two gunmen to and from the location. After dropping them off at the safe house, he took the car away and dumped it. The problem for Beggs was that there was an expensive radio in the hijacked car and he thought he would have it for himself. He didn't imagine the cops would think he had anything to do with what happened in a million years. They did, and when the radio was found in his car that was it.

The RUC took Beggs to Castlereagh for questioning and at first he stuck to his story, denying he had anything to do with the attack. When they made it clear that the radio was enough to convict him or his wife, he crumbled quickly. People mocked him for the mistake he made but I didn't and I still have respect for him.

The authorities could see that Northern Ireland was on the brink of total meltdown and something had to be done to try to stop it spiralling out of control. A decision was taken to round up the hardliners and on 28 October I was lifted and taken to Castlereagh. The cops knew they had to get the situation under control and brought out the big guns. It was the first time I met Derek Martindale.

To begin with, it was the usual scenario: they would try to put pressure on me and I would play along but give them nothing. Then they began to tell me the boss wanted to have a word with me. I wasn't really sure if they were trying to threaten me or what they were up to, so I waited to see what would happen.

When Martindale did show, it was clear he wasn't to be messed about with. He was the head of Northern Ireland's CID and when he walked into the cell you could sense his authority. The two coppers who were there changed their attitude instantly and it was crystal clear who the boss was. Immaculate in a perfect cashmere coat and a pristine white shirt, he leaned over the table and introduced himself as Detective Superintendent Martindale.

Until this point I was swinging back on my chair and hadn't moved when he came into the interview room. Now I raised my hand to shake his and said to him, 'It's nice to meet someone with the same rank as me.'

There was an audible gasp from the other two, who

didn't know what to do. As far as Martindale was concerned, it was time to stop messing about, so he cranked it up a bit. Quickly I reeled off a cheeky speech about how murder was wrong, it achieved nothing and the only way forward was for people to get round a table and talk.

Martindale stopped me in full flow, put his hand into his pocket and pulled out a diary. 'What did you say there?' he asked. 'I'm sure I heard a good quote in there. Something about murder being wrong. You were saying that murder was wrong.' Turning to the other two, he scoffed, 'That must be the quote of the year. Johnny Adair says that murder is wrong. I better get that down in the diary.'

Two days after I was taken into Castlereagh, Stephen Irwin and Jeffrey Deeney walked into the Rising Sun in Greysteel, near Londonderry, and opened fire with an AK-47 and a Browning 9mm pistol. They were dressed in boiler suits and wearing balaclavas. Drinkers in the bar at first thought it was a twisted Halloween joke. Seven Catholics and one Protestant were killed, bringing the total for the week to 23 dead.

Afterwards, the UFF issued a statement that said, 'This is a continuation of our threats against the Nationalist electorate that they would pay a heavy price for last Saturday's slaughter of nine Protestants.'

I was questioned about Greysteel and it was later wrongly claimed that during the interrogation I laughed. It was said I helped to mastermind the attack, because I'd been spotted in the area a week before it happened. The truth was I was visiting Norman Green junior at Magilligan Prison. A police surveillance team were on my tail but didn't pick me up on the way back to Belfast. It was nothing to do with me and a different UFF brigade carried it out.

Black October sent the whole of Northern Ireland back to the dark days of the 1970s. The whole place came to a standstill, the streets were deserted at night and people were scared to leave their homes. For the Republicans, I was public enemy number one.

The different factions had been competing to kill me since the start of 1993. At the beginning of the year I was taken to the Antrim Road and shown the graffiti on a wall. There in front of me in foot-high white letters was: 'Statement from New Lodge Road IRA. Johnny Adair is on the run. The IRA says that your day will come.' I knew it was the real deal and not something done by local thugs. The IRA now knew who I was and they were coming after me.

Twice IRA ASUs took over 54 Upper Glenfarne Street, which overlooked my own house on Hazelfield Street. It was ideal for them as the woman who lived in the property at the time was an OAP and almost blind. They won her over easily by pretending they were UVF and got themselves into position. One of the gunmen remained with her downstairs, armed with a handgun and a walkie-talkie, while the other two went upstairs and took up position with an AK-47. They thought their luck was in because my car was sitting outside the front door, but I was at the Belfast Motor Show. I rarely used my car, as most of the time I would be picked up by a driver.

While they were in the house, a relative of the OAP came

home who was a former member of the UDR. The IRA guys grabbed him and hauled him into the front room. They held a gun to his head and searched him, tied him up and continued to play the waiting game for me. For three hours, they sat there hoping to get a shot at me. Eventually they left empty-handed. When I spoke to the family afterwards, they said the assassination team had remained calm throughout their wait. The only sign of anything being out of place was when the tyres on their getaway car, which had been hijacked in the Ardoyne, screeched as they pulled away.

The operation had been carefully planned and it looked like Special Branch might have fed them a few lines. But at this stage I just thought I was being paranoid and putting too much weight on what the Branch had said to me in Castlereagh.

The second time the IRA took over Upper Glenfarne Street they were in for a surprise. The old woman had moved out and I'd moved Norman Green junior into the house. But when they made their move he was out and his wife was in. Again they claimed to be from the UVF and got themselves in place, but this time Norman's missus knew what was going on. They had just secured the magazine into the assault rifle when the front door opened and two men walked in. One of them was carrying a legally held firearm.

In an attempt to take control of the situation, the IRA men cornered the pair. The first was searched and given the all-clear, but as they prepared to search the second it was

obvious there was going to be trouble. The guns came out
and they all spilled out into the street. Moments earlier I'd
arrived home and walked past Norman's house unaware
what was going on.

For security reasons, I parked away from my own house
and had also recently changed my car. The gunman
hunched over his rifle didn't see me as I made my way
quickly across the road and into the house, where I stayed
for only a few moments. I asked Gina to order me a Chinese
meal and told her I was going to Norman's house. Grabbing
my keys off the high chair where my daughter Chloe was
sitting, I headed for the door. Then I heard guns going off.
I jumped over to the chair and pulled it and my little girl to
the floor. I could hear the shouting in the street warning me
not to come out. The IRA cell didn't have a getaway car in
the street and were shooting their way out to reach a pick-
up point.

I'm certain there were plenty of Republican gunmen who
would have been happy to go to prison for my murder.
They would have been carried shoulder-high through the
streets of the Ardoyne as heroes. It was no surprise they had
been prepared to take these risks.

I got the council to change the layout of Hazelfield Street
because gunmen could drive in one end and straight out of
the other. Workmen closed off one end of the road, creating
a cul de sac which made it more difficult for would-be
killers to carry out a drive-by shooting and escape quickly.

However, an INLA unit discovered that if they parked in
the street adjacent to mine there was a blind spot from

where they could launch their attack. I knew nothing about what they were up to until an RUC man came to the door and told me he had saved my life. The cops had driven by the gunmen as they sat in their car waiting for their chance. When the patrol vehicle doubled back, the unit panicked and screamed off. Eventually two of them were picked up.

On this occasion, the beat cops had saved my life, but I have no doubt there was collusion to have me killed. Intelligence that would make it easier for my enemies was certainly handed out and when that failed they sent 14th Intelligence, part of the army's special forces.

This move followed a UDA meeting in north Belfast. I wasn't there, but friends of mine were. An undercover intelligence team was in the area keeping an eye on what was going on. The intelligence services' operatives were brilliant, so that most of the time you had no idea they were there. In response, the UDA would have a counter-surveillance team in position and everyone was treated with suspicion.

That time a guy with a pony-tail was flagged up. He was hanging around outside where the meeting was going on. The guys decided to confront him and see who he was. They split into two teams and cornered him outside a bank. He wasn't flustered, saying he was from Tigers Bay and giving them a name of someone who lived there. Unfortunately for him, the name he used was of a guy known to them and they set about him viciously with a hammer. During the scuffle he went for his gun but it was taken from him.

Within minutes the area was swarming with coppers trying to rescue their undercover colleague. Some of the team were arrested but the guys who had the gun managed to escape. It had all got a bit messy. One of the guys who had given the cops the slip called me to let me know what had happened and that he'd got the officer's weapon. Taking a gun from a copper was a big problem for the security services. Their biggest fear was that the gun would be used in a murder and be discovered and that the facts would come out in a consequent court case. It had the potential to be a source of serious embarrassment.

Within half an hour of the phone call being made to me from the guy at the scene, the cops came through the door. The RUC's specialist unit sledgehammered in both the front and back doors of the house before turning the place upside down looking for any evidence. From the wire-tap on my phone, they had concluded that the gun was on its way to my home, and so were they guys who carried out the attack. This was their chance and they were going to have to move quickly. They got nothing.

Even though they had nothing on us at all, everyone in the house except the kids was arrested and taken to Castlereagh to be interrogated and held for 24 hours. I was sitting in an interview room when one of the coppers came in to have a word. It was clear that he was furious. Not only was one of his men fighting for his life but a gun had gone missing as well. He leaned over the table and said matter-of-factly, 'Get it back, it's a good fucking one. Get it back.'

After we were all released, some graffiti appeared on a wall in the Shankill saying, 'RUC dickheads, we got your 15-shot Smith & Wesson serial number XXXX.' That was pushing it too far, and a week after I was released the green light was given from somewhere high up the military chain of command for an undercover army assassin to take me out. As far as they were concerned, I was now the biggest threat in the Loyalist movement and I was rubbing their noses in it.

I was sitting in the house with a few of the guys from C Company when one of them noticed that a man had walked past the front of the house twice in ten minutes. My house was like Fort Knox, and I wasn't really bothered as anyone walking within 30 feet would be lit up by the standard security lights sited around the building, but the others were getting a bit agitated. Five minutes later, the guy reappeared and was caught in a beam of light from the side of the house.

The security forces had been inside my house on plenty of occasions, so they knew exactly what measures were in place to make sure that I was safe. This guy was trying to draw me out on to the street, and I obliged.

Instead of sending someone else to see what the guy was all about, I opened the door and stepped outside to deal with it myself. Just what he wanted. He was about 30 yards from the front door when I called after him, asking politely if I could help him. He stopped, turned and stared at me. Then, without a word, he walked off down the street. I was pissed off at his attitude and followed him, still calling to him. By now I was close enough to get a better look at the guy. He had long scruffy hair and was wearing a donkey jacket. A second time he came to a halt, eyeballed me and walked on without a word. I was furious that this tramp was giving me dirty looks outside my own house.

By the time we got to the end of the cul de sac and I was only about 20 feet from him, it began to dawn on me that I'd walked into a trap. The gunman was periodically turning and checking me out. In a split second he saw the fear in my eyes and realised he would have to make his move. As he spun round and started firing a handgun, all I saw were the flashes coming from the barrel. When the shots rang out, Donald Hodgen, who had followed me from the house, tried to get between me and the gunman. But Hodgen was 30 feet behind me.

Terrified, I ran for my life: it seemed that the gunman couldn't miss me from such close range. I scrambled to get back into my house, but the rest of the lads were trying to do the same thing. They assumed that, if Donald and I weren't dead now, we soon would be. My only option now was to pass my front door and try to get into a neighbour's house.

As I legged it, a car screeched down the road towards me, then another appeared and tried to corner me. The drivers, who I believe were the support unit for the gunman, didn't get out. They had been forced to show their hand and make sure the assassin wasn't coming under fire. I was half falling, half running to get away from the scene. My jeans and boots were shredded as I scrambled across the pavement and then jumped across the bonnet of the first car. As I ducked down and tried to find somewhere safe, I was violently sick. I got myself to Sham Millar's mum's door and kicked it in. I stayed there until the cops appeared on the scene and it had all calmed down. Somehow the gunman had missed me but had hit Donald in the chest and in the leg.

At this stage, we assumed that it was a Republican attack, but then I heard how the gunman had left the scene and I began to get suspicious. Someone who saw it all said that after firing he calmly turned and walked into the next street and was picked up by a white car that disappeared into the night. No panic: he just strode off to safety. But the full investigation didn't come until later on. First we had to get Donald to hospital. While we were there C Company hatched a plan to strike back at the Republicans straight away. The easiest response was to target a black-cab driver, as many were in the pay of the IRA. A taxi was called to the Mater Street Hospital and as it drew up two gunmen wearing baseball caps came over and fired through the side window. The guy survived.

Back at the house that evening, we turned on the news to see what was being reported about the two incidents. It was the lead item, and the reporter said, 'There have been two shootings in Belfast tonight. The first was in Hazelfield Street, where a man has been shot and wounded. It was carried out by an on-duty undercover soldier. Meanwhile, a Catholic taxi driver has been shot and wounded at the Mater Hospital.'

The security forces sent in the undercover soldier to kill me knowing that the previous week had given them an excuse for putting a bullet in my head. All the gunman had to say was that he was keeping tabs on me and was forced to challenge me in the street. That as things started to get heated he feared for his life, and as a result was forced to open fire. He was worried that he might end up in the same condition, if not worse than, the soldier the week before, for which incident I'd been arrested, of course. It was the perfect excuse, and my death would have been justified.

11

ABORTED

C Company continued to make its presence felt, despite the best attempts of its many enemies to take it out. As its reputation got better, so did the standard of people who wanted to join.

Derek Adgey was a disaffected Royal Marine whose work took C Company to another level. Sick of the reality of what was happening in Northern Ireland and on the mainland, he was determined to do something about it. The Belfast-born Protestant first tried to make contact with us by walking into a bar he knew was a UDA stronghold and asking if he could speak to me. When I heard about it, I smelled a rat. It was highly suspicious, someone appearing out of the blue with a Belfast accent, claiming to be a soldier and offering information. Yet I knew that, if he was genuine, he could be a gold mine of intelligence.

So I had his cover story looked into and it seemed to check out. But there was still the question of what would happen if we acted on anything he passed our way. Would the SAS be lying in wait for me if I turned up at an address? Before it went any further a meeting was arranged to establish how genuine he was. Adgey arrived and was strip-searched to make sure he wasn't wearing a wire or carrying a gun.

Adgey claimed he'd had it with going on patrol with 40 Commando, dealing with the IRA while knowing they were killing his colleagues and there was nothing he could do about it. In particular, he said, the IRA guys would have a dig at him about their notorious sniper 'One Shot Paddy', who was killing squaddies at will in south Armagh. Being stationed on the Falls, the middle of the Provos' heartland, and watching them get away with it was too much.

My impression was that Adgey was telling the truth and in the end it all came down to trust. Once the green light was shown, a network was set up to provide dynamite intelligence that would put the IRA on the back foot. He was the best thing to happen to the UDA in terms of intelligence-gathering since Brian Nelson. Any UDA unit that went out on the back of a contact sheet of images supplied by Nelson were given a clear run in and out of wherever their target was. Nobody was ever challenged or charged. Adgey wasn't at that level because he was doing it off his own back and that made him more dangerous to the Republicans. Nelson and his handlers had control of what he was supplying. Adgey was risking everything to get known IRA men off the street and there were no politics behind the scenes involved.

The information had to be handled carefully. Adgey was told that it could only be passed by letter and he was given an address in England where it was to be sent to his former girlfriend Jacqueline Newell. The 28-year-old mother of two would then relay the intelligence back to the Shankill, where it could be acted on.

Adgey was also given a mobile phone for emergency use. He was stationed in Fort Whiterock in west Belfast, so he knew everything that was going on: who was driving what, the safe houses that were being used and the movements of the army patrols. He was only to use the mobile if the security forces were about to move into an area where C Company was already under way. Adgey was coming into contact with the leading IRA men in Belfast every day, so when they were being stopped at checkpoints he took pictures of them. Nelson's stuff had been dated photocopies of old montages, whereas these mugshots were bang up to date.

Adgey's help allowed us to go after the figures at the top of the Republican tree. One operation, to kill a top Republican in the north called Brian Gillen, came tantalisingly close to success. Through Adgey, we learned that Gillen was regularly using a house in Riverdale Park South for meetings. A C Company team went to the street and sussed out the best address that could be taken over to allow a clear shot at the men as they went into their bolthole.

Once they had convinced the couple they were IRA men

waiting to hit an army foot patrol, access was gained to the house. It would have been almost impossible to take over the house and remain there if they had declared they were Loyalist gunmen. But in the heart of a Republican area there was no problem with IRA men getting the use of a house to shoot Brits.

The unit had included a scout in the street to keep an eye on what was going on. Just as Adgey promised, the men pulled into the estate in a Ford Sierra. The gunmen moved behind the door of the house, cocked their guns and waited for the moment to come. The team stopped outside the house and got out of the car. It was time to move. But then the radio crackled and a message came from the scout in the street: he had spotted an 18-strong army foot patrol just around the corner. If the ASU had attacked, it would have been carnage. By the time the squaddies were at a safe distance, the chance was gone. The C Company unit had held the owners of the house hostage for over an hour. They revealed who they really were and ordered them to tell Gillen how close he had been to the end.

This was C Company's first-ever house takeover and it ended up with the owner of the house being shot. He claimed that he was an IRA gunman and moaned about the way the operation was being carried out. When the mission was aborted, the C Company man blasted the IRA man with a machine gun as he sat on the sofa.

Although the attempt had failed, Adgey's information allowed C Company to move around Belfast knowing there was less chance of our walking into a security forces ambush, as Skelly's team had done in 1992. It also meant we could be more ambitious. Nothing was out of bounds.

Sinn Fein's headquarters, Connolly House, was on the Andersonstown Road, in the heart of Republican west Belfast, so any attack was going to be very difficult. The building itself was heavily fortified with high walls and protective fences. In February 1994, a decision was taken to instigate a small-scale operation to see how easy it would be to get in and out of the area and penetrate the building's security.

The idea was to leave a booby-trapped grenade that would be triggered using wire fishing line strung between a metal railing and a branch. The grenade was spray-painted to blend in with the colour of the fence and was attached at head height. C Company's Rab Bradshaw and Gary McMaster were dropped off at the Sinn Fein HQ in the middle of the night to set the trap. They got over the fence with no problem and placed the incendiary before making their getaway. But the following day, the thick wire, which had looked fine in the middle of the night, was spotted and the device was defused.

Although the plot was rumbled, C Company now had the confidence to get at Sinn Fein on their own patch. Days later, information came to us that Gerry Adams and senior members of the party were going to be meeting on a Saturday morning in Connolly House. It was just over seven miles from the Shankill, which doesn't sound a lot, but it was extremely difficult to move hardware any distance around Belfast with the security forces saturating the streets. A safe house in the Protestant stronghold of Suffolk, not far from the Andersonstown Road, and a garage were set up to make it easier for any ASU operations in the area.

With Adams scheduled to be in attendance, the big guns were brought out. Volunteers armed with an RPG7 rocket launcher and an AK-47 were embedded early on Saturday morning. Just after 11am, the rocket was fired, smashing through the meeting-room window and exploding. The building was also raked with gunfire. Yet nobody was hurt. It emerged that Sinn Fein had suspended all meetings as a security measure before the attack happened. They were up in arms and pointed to the British Army as the source of our intelligence.

Adams himself told the press, 'Loyalist death squads are operating with a high degree of intelligence information on individuals, offices and the movements of Crown force patrols.'

The truth was he had been scheduled to be there. C Company was getting to him. It was important to keep up the pressure.

Builders were brought in to fix the damage that had been inflicted on the building, but they weren't your usual labourers. Instead, IRA men carried out the work and two of them, we learned, were high-ranking members. No way would Sinn Fein have brought in anyone from the outside to carry out the work: it all had to be in-house.

On 18 February, a three-man unit, dressed in boiler suits and donkey jackets, pulled up opposite the headquarters and got out of their cars. They made their way to the front of the building, where the main team were working. As they got closer they dropped their sandwich boxes, whipped out machine guns and opened fire. After a short burst it was back in the cars and away. A few of the IRA workers were hit but nobody was killed. It was the third attack in two weeks and the Provos were getting more and more worried as the days went on.

There was nothing to stop C Company, which had now cemented itself as the most-feared unit in the UDA. It had come a long way from being a ragtag bunch who did little more than drink and racketeer. Now C Company was sophisticated enough to go after the biggest prize of them all: Gerry Adams. Killing the leader of Sinn Fein would rock the Republican movement to its core. It wouldn't be easy. Adams's security was permanently reviewed and his movements were always top secret. The layout of the street where he lived was also a nightmare: there was only one way in and out and at one end was a police station. Trying anything there was a virtual suicide mission. But it was worth the risk.

The plan was for two squeaky-clean C Company men not known to the police to be sent into the area in a clean car and to leave the wheels around the corner from Adams's house. They were to be armed with a fragmentation grenade. Anything more than that was too risky. A gun would be a giveaway and, even if it were to be disposed of later, there was always the chance that residue would remain at the scene. A grenade would be easier to get to the target and there was less of a risk of leaving forensic evidence.

The only other weapon was the local newspaper. For weeks, the classified section had been scoured to see if anything was for sale in Adams's neighbourhood. When something was found, it was ringed to give anyone found in the area a legitimate reason for being there. It wasn't going to stop the cops lifting anyone, but it would be a big help under questioning.

The grenade attack was duly launched. Adams wasn't there but his wife and son were left shaken by the attack. We were taking the fight literally to his front door, but it was clear that assassinating him at his home was going to be tough, so a surveillance team was put on to him to see what would turn up.

The first break was the address of his driver. Adams was ferried around in an armour-plated car and knowing where this could be found gave us a way to target him. A bomb could be placed under the car as it sat outside his driver's home at night. However, it became clear that rigorous checks of the car's underside were carried out before it went anywhere and any device was likely to be discovered.

All was not lost, though. Surveillance of the driver revealed that Adams was using a small fortified office at least twice a week. It was watched for almost a month and a routine was confirmed. Accurate and reliable intelligence was what was needed if the target was going to be killed. An ASU was selected and they were briefed about the plan. Adams's vehicle was to be rammed by a van with a sliding door. Immediately after the collision the team would open the customised door and unleash the arsenal. They would be armed with an RPG7, two AK-47s, a handgun and two grenades.

A getaway route to the Black Mountain, west of Belfast, had been selected and massive concrete bollards to block access to a country road removed. In the aftermath the cops would rule out the road and, by the time they guessed the team's route, they would be long gone. It was a perfect plan but it was never implemented. In the days before the bid was to be made, the members of the unit were arrested on another matter. By the time they were all out of custody, the scheme had been shelved and it was never revived.

Despite C Company's efforts, the UDA Inner Council weren't at all happy about the fast pace at which things were happening. Brigadiers including Alec Kerr, Billy 'The Mexican' McFarland, Gary Matthews and Tom Reid were desperate for us to slow down. McFarland was the only one I had any faith in. The rest of them were warning me that it was only a matter of time before I was locked up or killed. Slowing down was the last thing that I wanted to do, now that Sinn Fein/IRA were on the run. Their attitude confirmed my fears that most of them didn't have the stomach for the fight and, worse, that Special Branch were leaning hard on the Inner Council.

It later emerged that they were so concerned they plotted to kill me. When I was locked up for directing terrorism I was visited by a few people including Donald Hodgen and Winkie Dodds to tell me about the scheme. From the moment they walked in, it was clear they had something to say I wasn't going to like. When they said it was about an attempt on my life in 1994, at first I couldn't see what the fuss was all about. After all, it had happened plenty of times. Then they revealed that it was treachery from my own people. I couldn't believe it.

The plan had been to take me to the country on the pretext of picking up a stash of guns and kill me there. My car would be dumped on the Falls Road to make it look like it was a Republican plot. I was in and out of the Falls all the time, so it wouldn't have been hard for my people on the Shankill to believe I'd been caught there and murdered. Even without a body, the story would have been lapped up. While I had suspicions about Kerr, I trusted McFarland; we'd been on operations together and I would've had no problem going to a meeting with him.

The murder bid didn't come off because the guy they asked to do it refused. The other conspirators didn't have the bottle, so they approached him to pull the trigger. He knew how important I was to the movement and said there was no way he could do it. It was he who eventually told Winkie and the others what he had been asked to do. I was shocked that those guys had tried to have me killed. There is a good chance that Special Branch were putting pressure on them to have me dealt with.

C Company were running rings round the Branch and pulling operations together at the drop of a hat. Gerry Adams's cousin David Adams was targeted following the final edition of the news at 1am on a Friday. The bulletin revealed that five men, including Adams, had been snared by the cops on the way to murder Derek Martindale, the head of the CID. Adams and his unit were lifted in the east of the city in a hijacked van loaded with firearms and a coffee-jar bomb.

They were due to appear in the dock at Belfast Magistrates' Court the following day. The chances were, as it was a Saturday, the IRA guys would be the only accused to appear. At some stage, there would be a window of opportunity to get them as they were transported to and from the court.

C Company would set up an ambush along the route they would be taking, using a nearby house as a base. With the team armed with the rocket launcher and an AK-47, the IRA prisoners would be sitting ducks.

Within hours of the news, a safe house was selected and the early stages of the attack were about to be implemented. However, the plug was pulled when RUC officers spotted the UFF team entering the house. There was no way that the attack could go ahead. If anything happened, it would only be a matter of time before the people spotted the previous night were behind bars.

In April 1994, Adgey was arrested. He was caught because his mouth got too big and he told one of his colleagues how he was helping C Company go after top Republicans. At his trial in October 1995, he confessed to ten counts of soliciting murder and 12 of recording and collecting information. He told the court he hated the Provos and 'would rather they were killed than innocent Catholics'. He given was four years.

12

THE CRUM

I'd survived numerous attempts on my life from both outside and within the movement. And yet C Company had grown bigger and stronger and it was more important than ever that we had people at the top we could rely on, as the security services were subjecting us to ever-greater scrutiny. They were always on top of us, and me in particular. For our fight to succeed, we had to be able to rely on one another. And I needed someone with me I could trust never to let me down. Stevie 'Top Gun' McKeag was that man.

Stevie was one of the most ruthless and dedicated members of the UFF. He first came to my attention during a spat with the authorities at Crumlin Road Prison. The Victorian jail was a hell-hole, as I would later find out, with Loyalist and Republican remand prisoners forced to share the same wing. The conditions were horrific and cons were often given a hard time by the staff. When things came to a head, direct action was taken from the outside to put pressure on the guards.

Mac, who was military commander of C Company at the time, organised a team to go down and give a warning to the screws when they were leaving at the end of their shift. Guns were fired at them and a few grenades lobbed to make sure they knew C Company meant business. When I was told not long after about what happened, the report was that Mac had been the main man of action. I learned that in reality it had been Stevie, and he'd kept his mouth shut – exactly what was needed.

There were hundreds of men in C Company and until now Stevie had been no more than a face in the crowd. I didn't know much about him, so I made a point of having a word with him about what had gone down at the prison. He was desperate to get in at the sharp end and I could tell straight away he was trustworthy.

Unlike the IRA, we didn't have a sophisticated recruiting system or any training camps for new volunteers. It wasn't often that guys like Stevie put their hand up and offered to be part of an ASU. Weapons classes were held in safe houses around the Shankill and Stevie picked up everything very quickly. In no time he was stripping guns and making sure they were ready for action.

Stevie became known as 'Top Gun', for the simple reason that he was the best gunman in the UFF. It wasn't long before the cops got wind of who he was and were desperate to get him off the streets. He was lifted and charged with the murder of hairdresser Sean Hughes in September 1993. The gunmen were only wearing sunglasses to disguise their identity when they entered the shop off the Falls and killed the 40-year-old. Stevie was picked out of a line-up before the trial and it looked like he was going down for the killing. But he was to be cleared the following year when the judge ruled that he wasn't satisfied with the identification evidence. By that time, however, it would all be too late.

Stevie was on remand for well over a year, during which time Gary McMaster came through the ranks, and he was the man who would bring it all crashing down. I first met him through his brother, Keith, who was already a member of C Company. I liked Keith because he didn't question orders but just got on with it. Winkie and I went round to his house hours before he was supposed to go on an operation. It was the first time I'd been to his house in east Belfast and when we got there he had just got out of bed. The minute I walked in the door, I realised there was no way he could be sent out to kill.

Kids started appearing from everywhere as Winkie and I stood in the front room running through what was to be done. No disrespect to the guy, but he had nothing. If he went out on a job and got pulled by the cops, who was going to look after the kids? The Loyalist Prisoners' Association would provide some cash but it was never going to be enough. Keith was prepared to go on the operation and put C Company before his wife and kids, but

I wasn't going to let that happen. I had a word with Winkie and we came up with an excuse to get Keith off the job.

The UDA had a number of illicit drinking dens, or shebeens. Scattered all over the Lower Shankill, these were places where we could have a drink and socialise after hours. Keith ran one of them with Gary in a flat used otherwise only for social security cash drops. It was packed full of fridges and there was a sound system. On Friday, Saturday and Sunday nights, it was packed and raked in the cash. The cops made little effort to close down any of the shebeens and when they did board them up we just moved to another flat.

With Stevie McKeag in Crumlin Road Prison waiting to go to trial and Keith eased out of active operations, Gary quickly moved up the ranks. He was volunteering for every mission going and men like that were very hard to come by. It wasn't every day someone came up to you and offered to go head to head with the IRA.

Gary was desperate to be part of C Company's inner circle. Men were joining the UDA mainly for me and not just because they believed what we were fighting for. When I gave Gary the nickname 'Captain', within days he'd got it tattooed on his arm next to a clenched 'Red Hand of Ulster'. That's how badly he wanted to belong. But, as he moved so quickly through the ranks of the UDA, he missed out on a lot of the training. It was my job to educate the men on dealing with Special Branch interrogation techniques if they were taken to Castlereagh. But Gary was straight in at the deep end.

THE CRUM

C Company had the IRA on the run with a wave of attacks on Sinn Fein councillors, property and known Provo haunts. An RPG7 team was giving the cops sleepless nights and Gary was at the heart of their operations. On the team's first outing, he and Rab Bradshaw were sent to a notorious Republican boozer called the Rock Bar, where Brian Gillen was supposed to be holding a meeting. The ASU poured out of the car about 100 yards from the pub and Rab took aim with the RPG7. He squeezed the trigger and waited for the explosion. But the rocket missed. To make matters worse, the 25-foot flame blew back from the launcher and scorched the getaway car. Despite the damage done to the car, the unit managed to get out of the area. The motor had been brought in at the last minute because the first one was too small for the rocket to fit in.

From there Gary was involved in everything: house takeovers, bomb attacks and stashing a lot of our arsenal.

But cracks began to appear and he got sloppy. Gary was messing about with a gun he was supposed to be hiding when it went off and shot him in the hand. He was too embarrassed to say anything to us and went to the hospital. The staff didn't fall for the excuse he gave them and the cops were called. When he was patched up, the detectives leaned on him and told him he had better start feeding them information or face charges.

Days later, the cops cornered him again, this time as part of a team who had taken over a house and were getting ready to raid a post office. When they took him in for questioning he cracked, implicating himself and half of C

Company in 32 charges, including murder and possession of guns.

The coppers scored another victory when they lifted a C Company ASU, just as they had Skelly's team two years before. Gary 'Smickers' Smith, Ricky Calderwood, Glen Esdale and Rab Bradshaw were stopped on the way to target INLA man Gino Gallagher. Esdale belonged to the south Belfast UDA but his home in the Suffolk area in the west was the perfect place for us to use as a base. However, this time he organised another safe house for the move on Gallagher. It was a mistake. The owner told the cops, who swooped quickly and picked up the lot of them. The cops knew it was a serious blow and were certain it was the end for C Company.

When the big push to get the rest of us came, on 16 May 1994, I had no idea how serious it was. There had been rumblings that the RUC were planning to employ a new means to get paramilitary leaders off the streets: using the charge of 'directing terrorism'. It didn't concern me, because every day a new tactic was being bandied about in an attempt to scare us.

It was just before 7am when the Land Rovers arrived in the street. It seemed like the usual raid and there was nothing to suggest the end was near. After they completed their search of the house, I was taken for questioning to Gough Barracks rather than Castlereagh. I'd been working with the UVF's Billy Wright in Armagh, so I assumed this was the reason for the change of venue. The strange thing was that Gina had been arrested and was also being questioned in Gough.

THE CRUM

It was only two days later, when I was allowed to see my solicitor, that I realised how much trouble we were in. Most of the main players in C Company had been lifted, but they were being held in Castlereagh. With me isolated miles away in Armagh and McMaster giving a statement, the cops had plenty of material to frighten them with. Normally, if I was in with a load of guys I could speak to them through the bars and shout encouragement to them. This time they were on their own.

During their questioning of me, the cops were trying a different tack. They started to produce things seized from my house. Combat jackets, baseball bats, pickaxe handles and UDA regalia were pulled out and shown to me: anything linking me to paramilitary activity. I had plaques on the wall in my house from other battalions of the UDA and from the Loyalists Prisoners' Association, and these items were being used as evidence now. The more that was brought out, the more concerned I got. Maybe they were building towards a directing terrorism charge, I thought.

UDA Inner Council brigadiers, especially Billy McFarland, had been terrified about new legislation being brought in. The idea was that the Director of Public Prosecutions would be able to prove that certain godfathers were in charge of paramilitaries. A court would be shown who the accused associated with, and this information would be backed up with an investigation into personal finances and any other links to the organisation of which he was supposed to be in charge. I relaxed a bit, knowing I didn't have a mountain of cash tucked away, and I was careful the rest of the time.

But I had no idea how long they had been looking into me or the lengths they had gone to. The security services had pulled together a huge amount of circumstantial evidence in their efforts to paint a picture of me as being at the top of the Loyalist terrorist tree. Officers were instructed to get me to talk when I was stopped at roadblocks or at any opportunity they got. They knew I was cocky and would sound off. Although it wasn't enough to get a conviction on a particular charge, it put me in the frame and that was what they wanted. When they asked me where I was going, I'd tell them that I was 'off to make the headlines for the news tonight'. It all added up. They even used the fact that the IRA had tried to kill me as evidence that I was the top man.

A massive team that included all levels of the security services in Northern Ireland were involved in the case. The prosecution had more than a thousand statements to be used against me in the trial. Yet, despite all the people involved, Jonty Brown was the officer who was ultimately given all the glory for bringing me down.

Ever since I'd met Brown when he interviewed me about the Finucane murder, he'd taken a special interest in me. He regularly came to my house to see what was going on, and a number of times he warned me that the IRA were stepping up their operations against me. I have no idea whether he was telling the truth or not. It made no difference to him.

Brown seemed to hang about and see what was going on.

He was desperate to impress me. I recall he showed me a picture of an active IRA gunman called Kevin Mulgrew. I had no idea what he looked like and Brown knew that. First he produced pictures of his kids from his wallet, then came the snap of Mulgrew. 'This man is paranoid and that's what keeps him alive,' he said. 'Remember, Johnny, back alleys and black taxis. He doesn't trust his own people and that's how he travels.'

During interrogation he often left my file on the table long enough for me to get a look. Inside there was top-grade intelligence, not just on me, and the notes also revealed where this came from and what moves were being made.

But there was no sign of Brown at Gough. It was top brass who were piling on the pressure, and they were using all the tricks in the book. Surveillance teams had been watching me and spotted me in the company of a woman named Jackie 'Legs' Robinson.

Gina already suspected there was something going on between us. She had spotted Jackie watching me in a club but I'd managed to bluff my way out of it. The cops weren't going to let me off the hook so easily. Gina had been questioned by detectives in the past and I was confident she would be able to handle Gough. After every interview, I went to the bathroom and from there I was able to shout up to her and make sure everything was all right. There were no problems to begin with and I knew she was dealing with what they were throwing at her. But on the second day when I shouted up and asked if everything was OK, all I got back was an abrupt 'aye'. I could tell from her voice it wasn't. During her interrogation, the detectives had asked her if she knew who Jackie 'Legs' was. She told them nothing and was released without charge. But it was all the confirmation she needed about Jackie.

At the end of seven days' questioning, I was taken to Crumlin Road Court and charged with directing terrorism. Cops ringed the courtroom: they weren't taking any chances. My solicitor, Billy McNulty, put it to the judge that the evidence the prosecution planned to use against me was mostly inadmissible. The statements the police claimed I'd given had been obtained when I wasn't under caution and therefore they couldn't be used in court.

After speaking to Billy, I was less concerned about the charge of directing terrorism. The best thing they seemed to have was details on the amount of times I'd changed my car. To me it all seemed incidental. The IRA had named me in a statement, so I must be the main man?

I had bulletproof glass in the house and regularly changed my car for security reasons. What did that prove? Nothing, as far as I was concerned. However, behind the scenes the Director of Public Prosecutions had been working hand in hand with the security services and making sure they knew exactly what would be needed to make the charge stick. As I was taken down, I gave the thumbs-up to Gina and the supporters who had made it to the court. I knew I was facing a long stretch on remand and I would need to use that time to prepare myself for the fight.

Word spread quickly through the wings of Crumlin Road Prison that I was on my way. In the Maze convicted terrorists more or less had the run of the place but in the 'Crum' it was much tougher. The cells were damp and stinking. Prisoners were forced to slop out and the beds came complete with old woollen army covers. There were no telephones or televisions, both standard in the Maze.

For years there had been a battle for Loyalist and Republican prisoners to be housed in different wings. In November 1991, Robert Skey and Colin Caldwell were killed in the dining hall of the jail's C Wing when an IRA bomb went off. The 8oz high-explosive device, planted behind a radiator, showered the room in shrapnel and cut the two Loyalists down. It made no difference to prison policy. The only concession the authorities made when I arrived was to move four Provos from my wing who were charged with attempting to murder me. They figured there might be a bit of friction.

The screws took every opportunity to make life difficult. When I first arrived, I had rings through my nipples which they insisted be removed. I refused and was sent to my cell. I thought it was the end of the matter until the riot squad came to get me with a hacksaw to cut them off. I handed them over pretty quickly.

While I was upset about being locked up, at least I was on the remand wing with a lot of men from my unit. I was only in a few days when we sat down and discussed what we were going to do about the segregation issue. There was every chance I could be remanded for two years in the Crum and I wasn't the only one facing an age stuck there. A delegation of UDA and UVF prisoners decided we wanted to be moved to the Maze. The only way that was going to happen was if we wrecked the place. If it was left in a bad enough state, they would have to transfer us.

I was being held on B Wing, which had a very small exercise yard, and the rest of the prisoners were in A Wing, where the yard was much bigger. The two adjacent areas were divided by a large fence and a gate secured by a huge Chubb lock. The first phase of the plan was to force the lock and then all climb up on the roof. In turn we tried to get it open, but before long the screws realised what was going on and addressed us through the Tannoy system. Stop what you're doing, they barked, or we'll send in the riot squad to deal with you.

It was looking like a lost cause when the lock suddenly gave way and, after negotiating the rolls of barbed wire laid out between the two yards, we were through. The scenes of elation must have looked like we'd won a war. But we still had to get on to the roof.

In the yard was a large shelter where the prisoners went when it was raining. A squad of cons gathered round it and began rocking it until it had been loosened so much it could be removed from its foundations. Once that was done, its timber frame was flipped up and placed on the side of the wall, acting like a ladder to the first level of the roof. This was repeated to get us all up on to the top tier. In all, 104 prisoners made it.

By now the riot squad were below, waiting to move in if negotiations failed. It was a brilliantly sunny evening and the Crum was right next to the Lower Shankill Estate. All

John Gregg standing by my shoulder on my release from prison.

UFF volunteers 2nd Batt C Coy pose for calendar picture.

Press Eye Ltd, Belfast

Above; Being released from the Maze, September 1999.

Left: With Portadown Loyalist Gary Fulton at the Drumcree stand-off, July 2000.

Press Eye Ltd, Belfast

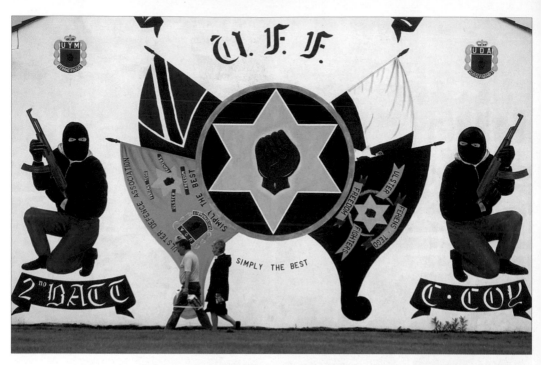

Top: UFF mural.

Bottom left: UDA mural.

Bottom right: Female member of the UFF, August 2000.

Press Eye Ltd, Belfast

Top: Members of the UFF Negotiating Team on Decommissioning on the Shankill Road (*left to right*) Winky Dodds, Jackie McDonald, John White, me, John Gregg, December 1999.

Bottom: The bullet-riddled taxi containing the body of John Gregg, February 2003.

Top pic: Press Eye Ltd, Belfast

Top: Ulster Prisoner's Aid building left gutted after an attack that took place as part of the feuding.

Bottom: Workmen clean up the damage caused to houses on the Lower Shankill wrecked in the feud between the UDA and the UVF, September 2000.

Top: With my son Jay and our dogs.

Bottom: With political spokesperson John White.

Press Eye Ltd, Belfast

With Gina outside our Shankill Road home the day I was released from prison.

Press Eye Ltd, Belfast

our friends and family came out and could see us from the street and there was even a Loyalist flute band from Scotland knocking out a few tunes. Any time the prison officials tried to coax us down, they were met with a barrage of bricks and roof tiles from above. It didn't matter if the riot squad fired on us with plastic bullets or got out the water cannon, we were staying there until the authorities cut us some sort of deal.

Normally, in the situation we were in, all the rioters would eventually be rounded up, battered by the riot squad and charged. On this occasion, the governor agreed that if we came down our grievances would be listened to, no heavy-handed tactics would be used and there would be no charges. A deal was struck and we came down, but it didn't last. It was decided we had to go for the final push.

At 8pm, all Loyalist prisoners were going to try to break through their cell walls. These were three feet thick and all the beds were bolted to the floor, so they couldn't be used as a lever. It didn't matter: we were going to give it a go. If we managed to get into a neighbouring cell with a Provo and have a scrap, they would have to segregate us.

I was desperate to get digging and tried to prise the bed from the floor, but a screw heard what I was up to and came into my cell and grilled me. He noticed I'd damaged the bed and hauled me out of the cell. But, instead of being moved to solitary, I was locked up with a UVF con, doubling our chances of getting through the wall.

At 8pm, the mass assault on the wall began. There were two Republican brothers in the next cell, and when they heard the banging they shouted, 'Don't be so stupid, Adair. You're never coming through the wall.' But, as the distant taps became louder thuds, they began to panic. Maybe I was going to make it through the wall and, if I did, what was I going to do to them? Soon they started screaming at the screws to come and rescue them. Eventually, all Provos on the wing were moved, but we didn't stop. It was a hellish night. With the Republicans off the wing, the electricity was cut. My body was aching and my hands were covered in blisters. The air was thick with dust from the smashed bricks, making it difficult to see or breathe.

At four in the morning, a riot squad of screws came through the door. The team in full body armour smashed their way in and knocked the shit out of me. There was no deal now and the gloves were off. My cell mate was screaming for mercy. I was held to the floor by knees in my back and pressure on the side of my face. The cuffs were clamped on as tight as possible and my arm was twisted as far up my back as it could go. For over an hour, I was left secured to the bed until the rest of the wing was brought under control. The pain was horrific but the screws left me there until a doctor arrived and ordered the cuffs be removed.

Our mission was accomplished. The prison was ripped apart and the next day we were moved to the Maze.

13

A BETTER CLASS OF PRISON

After 16 months on remand in the Maze, my big day came. The trial was going to be a big occasion as the authorities were delighted that they had got me. They were determined that nothing should go wrong and that my capture should signal the end of C Company.

The trial, due to start on 6 September 1995 at Belfast Crown Court, would be the most expensive in Northern Ireland's history, costing £1 million. It would be presided over by Mr Justice Anthony Campbell and was expected to go on for more than three months. In the weeks and months leading up to the trial, the prosecution played hardball. Their time and money were directed towards one outcome: a guilty verdict and a 30-year sentence. There was no way I was going to beat it.

Some of the evidence might have been a bit weak, but

there were over a thousand statements against me, most of them from police officers. I knew that and they knew I knew it. So they offered me a deal. I could take 20 years. My legal team knocked it back. Eventually, we settled for 16. There was no peace process at the time and I have no doubt I would have got 30 if I'd fought it.

On the day I was due in the dock, there was a buzz around the Maze. The previous night I'd gathered the men and told them I'd done a deal, but there was still an air of anticipation. I was dressed in a football shirt and jeans for my day in the dock. The wardens slapped on the handcuffs and took me to the prison van that was waiting to take me on the 30-minute drive to the court. The trip was rough and bumpy as the convoy raced me to Belfast. The first stop was a holding cell in the Crum, where I sat on my own and waited to be taken through the underground tunnel and into the court. I knew what was coming. Sixteen years. I had no regrets and I vowed to be strong in the dock. There were men in the Maze who had sacrificed everything for the UDA and me. I had to take the sentence on the chin.

A team of prison security guards came to take me into the court. I was handcuffed to one and flanked by at least four as we walked through the underground tunnel that connected the prison to the court-house. It was dingy inside and there was a stink of damp. Before going into Court One, I was held in another cell. Billy McNulty came to see if I was all right and told me the cops had stopped a lot of my supporters getting in. Then it was time to go.

I walked up the stairs and sat down behind the

bulletproof glass. The excitement was eating away at my stomach. As I looked around the courtroom, the first thing I noticed were the police. They were mob-handed. No risks were being taken today. All eyes were on me, trying to gauge a reaction. By then, I'd been in prison for over a year and the press were desperate to see how I was coping.

Flanked by two officers, I heard an inventory of the items seized from my home: 74 UFF wall calendars, a list of 60 UFF remand prisoners and a photograph of armed and masked men featuring UFF and UDA emblems. They also revealed that I had been recorded saying, 'I tried my hand at everything but no go. So I had a go at terrorism. The ball's at my foot in the whole of the North of Ireland. If I say it goes it goes, and if I say stop it stops. I have some … power, I'll tell you.' There was another tape of me saying, 'I rule by fear. The threat of one behind the ear keeps them in line.'

Crown Prosecutor Pat Lynch finished his speech by describing me as 'dedicated to his cause, which was nakedly sectarian in its hatred of those it regarded as militant Republicans – among whom he had lumped almost the entire Catholic population'.

After just over an hour, I was sentenced to seven years for membership of the UFF, seven years for membership of the UDA and 16 years for directing terrorism. As I was taken down, I clenched my first and thrust it into the air and shouted, 'I applaud the dedication of all the young men of the second battalion.'

Then it was back to the Maze to start my sentence. It

could have been worse, as the prison was like a working men's club and we could do what we wanted.

The jail was divided into eight H blocks, with a total population of anywhere between 750 and a thousand which was split fifty-fifty between Loyalists and Republicans. When I first arrived at the Maze, it had seemed like a different planet from Crumlin Road. The attitude of the wardens was amazing: they couldn't do enough for you. I was used to screws doing everything to make my life a misery. In the Maze I was on first-name terms with them, and I was allowed to wear a watch and keep my earrings on. A head count was carried out once a day, but apart from that we were pretty much left to ourselves. Food was delivered to the block three times a day and prisoners were allowed to dish it out themselves. Cell doors were never locked and access to the exercise yard wasn't restricted. Most of the main players from C Company were all together under the same roof 24 hours a day and I think the shortest sentence of any of the convicted prisoners was nine years.

But events on the outside made the start of the sentence tough. Before my trial the IRA decided to see what the UDA had left. A purge of leading Loyalists was carried out, killing three of the organisation's main men. The chairman of the Ulster Democratic Party, Raymond Smallwoods, was shot several times as he left his home in July 1994. A five-strong ASU took over a house, keeping an elderly couple hostage overnight as they waited for him to appear. Two sawn-off shotguns and the getaway car used in the attack were later found dumped behind a pub.

Later the same month, Raymond Elder and his close associate Joe Bratty were gunned down as they walked out of the Kimberley Bar and headed for their car. Elder had previously been charged with the murder of five men at Sean Graham's betting shop in February 1992, though the charges were later dropped. Nationalists believed Bratty was also involved. Two gunmen armed with AK-47s jumped from the back of a white van which was parked in front of their car and opened fire. The two of them tried to make a break for it but were cut down as they fled. More than 50 rounds were discharged and as the two men lay on the ground the IRA men walked up and finished them off from close range before jumping into a waiting car.

The ASU was chased by an RUC patrol to the Lower Ormeau Road, where a crowd came on to the streets and covered for the gunmen as they vanished among the bodies. The deaths of all three men were a terrible blow to Loyalists, and, for me, being able to do nothing about it was even worse.

I had a lot of time for Bratty, mainly because, like me, he had survived a number of gun and bomb attacks. It was a Sunday when news came through of his murder, and I had a meeting to discuss what was to be done. I was certain there would be revenge that night for what had happened. Donald Hodgen and Winkie Dodds were running the show and I was confident they would make sure the IRA's actions didn't go unanswered. One of the other leaders turned to me and said, 'That's Johnny Adair thinking. Those men are not you.'

Despite what he said, I was sure something would happen. But, as the weeks went by, the guns remained silent. The Inner Council were called to the prison to explain why nothing was going on and it was obvious none of them was interested. The IRA were flexing their muscles to see what the UFF had to offer with me behind bars and they got their answer: nothing. C Company still had the men but with nobody at the helm they were going nowhere. It hurt me badly. Three men had been murdered and there was nothing I could do about it. Special Branch were right, the guys left on the Inner Council were only good for keeping a lid on me. If they weren't going to do anything on the outside, it would have to be done on the inside.

At visiting times, Loyalist prisoners walked past the entrance to the Republican visiting room. A plan was put together for two Browning 9mm handguns and grenades to be smuggled into the prison and an assault carried out as the Provos met their families. A two-man team was selected but it never came off. I think the reason, in the end, was that no one wanted to spray bullets around a room full of women and children.

It certainly wasn't because of a lack of weaponry. It was easy smuggling contraband on to the wings. Most visitors were given a very cursory search and the political representatives weren't searched at all. Alcohol was hidden in balloons and passed to prisoners during visits. Mobile phones were also handed over. I think the security forces were happy there was communication between paramilitaries behind bars and on the outside, because they could listen in and hear what was being planned.

H-block had four wings with the screws having the middle part. The Loyalist wing was searched twice a year and even then there was a 30-minute warning beforehand so any contraband could be stashed away. On one search, the tail of a sniffer dog wagged and knocked over a UDA mug sitting on a table in my cell. I didn't care at all but the guy insisted on writing me out a cheque for £15. Prisoners were given just a gentle pat-down, whereas in Crumlin Road it was a full strip-search.

Facing at least 12 years locked up, I knew it was important to find a distraction to occupy the mind. For me it was body-building. I went in 10 ½ stone and came out 13 ½ stone of solid muscle with a 46-inch chest. I was disciplined about what I was doing. I was taking 27 different pills, a protein drink every three hours 24 hours a day and was eating the right things. As the prison meals weren't up to much, proper food had to be smuggled in. Members of the UDP came to see us every Monday and let us know what the latest was on the peace process. One of the team had a false leg and would stuff it full of sirloin steaks, chicken, steroids and whatever else we needed. He looked the part, decked out in his suit, and was never searched.

At the weekend, and sometimes during the week, there were all-night parties. The prison authorities provided us with disco lights and a decent PA system and there was always a steady supply of ecstasy, acid and dope. There was never any danger of running out of drink or drugs. The only thing to get us down after a night on the Es was the lack of women. At 3am the only place you were going was back to your cell.

That's not to say that sex was totally off the menu. The best way to get some was during a private prison visit. They were normally supposed to be used for inmates who were having family trouble, but it wasn't difficult to persuade the governor you needed one.

You were provided with a small room away from the normal visiting centre and at the end of the corridor a warden would keep a distant eye on the situation. The room had nothing apart from a table and a couple of chairs. Everyone knew what the private visits were really being used for but a blind eye was turned. You had to take a coat down with you and a couple of pins as there was no door for the cubicle. The screw would sit in his small office until your time was up and when he came to get you every step would be a stomp down the corridor. It was only 15 feet but he made sure the approach was loud enough for you to know it was time to get yourself sorted out.

It was also going on in regular visits and even with other people in the room. You were given your own cubicle and, when we got the screws to build them up higher, it gave you a bit more privacy. A few of the prisoners had to be warned because they were making too much noise and there were kids in the room. Everyone was at it.

The drug taking was making a few people on the outside unhappy and they tried to get me to stop it. But I was having none of it. The same men who were calling for it to be stopped were getting loaded and chasing women at the weekend. Was it supposed to be all right for them on the outside to enjoy themselves but not for us? No chance. The men in the Maze had given their all for the Loyalist movement and anything that made their time easier was all right by me. What else were they supposed to do? When a consignment came in, it was divided up and handed out equally. Not everyone took drugs but there were a lot who did. Even the wardens had a dabble after their drinks had been spiked. Hooch was at one time the big thing behind bars but it took ages to make. There were no problems like that for us, with drink readily available.

The boredom was sometimes chronic and resulted in all sorts of mayhem. Lighter fuel used to be stockpiled and when there was enough a stash of petrol bombs would be made. The wing would be divided into two groups and the bombs lobbed at each other. Fire-hose fights were another favourite, although often the whole wing would end up flooded.

A bookmaker's was also set up in the canteen. Televisions were rigged up on a makeshift gantry high above the ground to allow all the men to see live horseracing or watch the results come in on Teletext. Proper betting slips and miniature pens were laid out on tables in front of two guys taking bets for big money.

The first time I walked in, there were thousands of pounds on the bookies' desk and the punters were transfixed by the screen, waiting for the latest race. It could have been any branch of William Hill in the country, were it not for the prison walls. There were a few smiling faces, but many more disgruntled punters cursing their horse and scrunching up a useless slip. There was even a cell set aside as a tattoo parlour, complete with the proper equipment, full set of inks and designs displayed on the wall for cons to pick from. One of the prisoners on another wing did a great Sunday roast and every weekend the wardens would send a minibus to pick a couple of us up and take us round to be fed.

Our relationship with the wardens was so good I managed to negotiate televisions, stereos and videos for every cell on the wing. The authorities had budgets to meet and there were loads of ways the prisoners could help them do that. None of us used the carbolic soap, razors or standard-issue toothpaste as our families would bring us decent stuff when they visited. There was a potential killing to be saved for the governor. If we helped them tuck away a few quid, some of the cash could be spent on the prisoners. So we had the kitchen kitted out with bigger fridges and deep-fat fryers were brought in. Of course, some of the stuff went missing. Every Monday, some of the political team would walk out of the prison with hi-fis and portable televisions tucked under their arm. As long as we didn't push our luck too much, it could be done.

Some of the prisoners had budgies on the wing but I wanted a dog. I sent word out to a contact and a visitor was sent up with a drugged Pomeranian stuffed down his tracksuit bottoms. I knew if I got it on to the wing the chances were I would be allowed to keep it. Sadly, the smuggling operation was rumbled when the dog woke up and the prison officers heard it whimpering.

New arrivals were made to face the 'boss of bosses' when they arrived. It meant they were marched into a cell where I would be waiting with a couple of hooded men and subjected to what they thought was an interrogation. In reality, it was just an opportunity for us to wind them up.

One of those who ended up on the wing was a Securicor driver called Keith Winward. He was a former infantryman with the Green Howards and had settled in Northern Ireland after doing three tours of duty. In April 1996, he claimed to the UDA that he could stage a robbery of his own cash security van, although I didn't get to hear about it until he was locked up.

He suggested that a team should burst into his family's house in Taughmonagh and pretend to take them hostage while he was on a shift. A call would be put through to him demanding he follow the instructions he was given or his relatives would get it. The scheme didn't convince anyone; they all thought he was just shooting his mouth off. It was common for people to come to us and boast they could do this and organise that but there was also the chance it could be a trap set by the security services.

Eventually, it was decided to give Winward the benefit of the doubt and the heist was set in motion. He turned out to be too smart for his own good. With the van carrying £1.5 million, making this the biggest bank robbery in the country at the time, he drove it straight to the drop-off point without looking at the instructions he had been given. His co-driver, Keith Dixon, thought something was out of place and told the cops Winward found the drop-off point without any guidance at all.

At the end of Winward's 11-day trial, the judge said, 'It was a highly organised and well-executed robbery,' and sent him down for 15 years.

A massive RUC operation later failed to recover any of the money, despite at one stage dredging an entire lake at Malone Golf Club. Securicor bosses issued a writ against Winward in an attempt to get their money back in November 2000, but by then the UDA had fleeced him of the lot. I told him he was being ripped off but he didn't listen. By that stage, he'd had toy soldiers smuggled into the Maze which he used to line up on a table and tell us he was explaining the tactics the cops and the army used. He became a nuisance on the wing and in the end he was taken out at the request of other prisoners.

There was a calendar of events we celebrated on the wing, such as Remembrance Day and 12 July. Replica AK-47s were made from wood and volunteers wore full military gear. For 12 July, we spent the night drinking around a bonfire and listening to a flute band.

At Christmas, we were allowed to have the family visit to the prison for the day and have a party. The gym and the exercise area were transformed into a winter wonderland with an officer dressed up as Santa handing out presents to the kids. One year, though, an IRA man exploited the trust and escaped dressed as a woman when the family members left at the end of the day.

It wasn't all fun and games. Some prisoners had to be disciplined. One con was out on parole and was trying to mess about with a lifer's wife. He knew what prisoners went through worrying about what their partners got up to while they were locked up. There was no excuse. Word got back to the Maze about what was going on and the men were brought together and asked what they thought should be done.

When the offending prisoner got back, he was given a kicking by the guy whose wife he was messing about with. Later on, he was called for and forced to explain himself to the rest of the inmates in the canteen. He thought his punishment was over and he was just going to get a dressing-down. Instead, two masked men walked in behind him clutching table legs and got stuck into him. When they were done, he was tossed on to a hospital trolley, both his legs smashed to bits, and pushed out into the exercise yard, where the prison officers called to collect him. There was no room for him on our wing and he was taken to an ordinary criminal jail.

Another guy tried to cut a deal with the cops when he was lifted. He told them that for a reduction in his sentence he would spy on me in the Maze and tell them everything that was going on. Unfortunately for him, we found out and he ended up slipping in the shower block.

There was little trouble between us and the Provos because it was rare we actually came into contact with them. But the Shankill bomber Sean Kelly did get a beating when he bumped into two Loyalists on the way to a visit. Afterwards, word was sent back from the Republicans that Kelly was to be left alone. They claimed he was really struggling with his sentence and coping with what he had done.

The only time there was any real trouble between ourselves and the prison staff was when they discovered an IRA escape tunnel in 1997. They were furious and the result was a massive programme of changes in the way the prison was run. Loyalist prisoners didn't have an escape policy but it didn't matter: we were going to be punished just like the Provos. When it was made clear we weren't going to co-operate with the new regulations, all visits and paroles were cancelled. All communications between us and the authorities broke down, so the only answer was a rooftop protest. The riot squad were sent in and it looked like it was going to escalate into a major incident. However, a UFF statement was released to the press declaring that there would be retaliatory strikes against the Northern Ireland Office and the Prison Service unless the riot squad were stood down. Within minutes, they backed off.

Being off the streets was in some ways a relief for me. The IRA had been coming after me every day and I knew there was a good chance they would get me at some point. I couldn't go on for ever hoping that the AK round was going to miss or the bomb wouldn't detonate properly. Behind bars I knew it would be easier for me for a while.

Then Gina said she was going to leave me, and, although my initial response was to tell her to go, soon I was all over the place. The biggest fear in being locked up was wondering what your wife or girlfriend was up to. So, if you got a big sentence, it was best just to let go: there was no point in both of you doing the time.

On top of that, everyone on the wing came to me with their problems and they all expected solutions. There was no time to think about myself. The pressure got so bad I had to go to the prison hospital for a week. My life was racing at 100 mph and it was suffocating me. Too often I was putting other people in front of myself and my family. Sam came to see me and told me I had to sort my head out. He was the only one allowed to visit. Every day he would bring letters the lads had written to me giving me support and telling me how much they appreciated me. It was their support that gave me the strength to pull myself together.

In 1997, I was left stunned by the murder of Billy Wright inside the Maze. He'd been the leader of the UVF in mid-Ulster and was as hardline as they come. I'd had some dealings with him and had a great deal of time for him. Wright had fallen out with the UVF after the 1996 Drumcree dispute, when the Orange Order were prevented from walking down the Nationalist Garvaghy Road.

A Catholic taxi driver named Michael McGoldrick was murdered on Wright's orders and eventually the Orangemen were allowed to walk. But the killing of McGoldrick was seen as a step too far by the leadership of the UVF and Wright's unit was disbanded. He responded by setting up the Loyalist Volunteer Force in his Portadown stronghold, where he had massive support.

At a rally he told the crowd, 'It has broken my heart to think fellow Loyalists would turn their guns on me.'

This new faction alarmed the authorities, who were sure it would result in trouble, especially as they knew Wright didn't support the peace process. It was confirmed by his representative, Lindsay Robb, who read out a statement at Stormont to the effect that they weren't on board. Robb was the first to be taken off the streets and was given ten years for conspiracy to run guns. He was to be stabbed to death in Glasgow after his release.

During Robb's trial, MI5 officers, who gave their evidence from behind screens, were ridiculed by defence lawyers for their inaccuracy. A private police report later advised the security services to improve their training methods. But the spooks, worried that Wright could sink the whole peace process, weren't going to give up. In March 1997, he was given eight years for threatening to kill a woman and intimidating her son.

When he was charged, he told the officer, 'With all my heart and with total honesty, I am innocent of both charges and genuinely believe they are sinister and political.'

Even if he was guilty, it was a very heavy sentence. The following month, he was transferred from Maghaberry Prison, where ordinary, decent criminals were held, to the INLA's H6 block at the Maze. From the start, it was clear that it was a mistake and there would be only one outcome.

Two days before Christmas, Christopher 'Crip' McWilliams shot Wright dead as he sat in a minibus waiting to be transferred to the visiting area. It is thought that INLA prisoners acted on the spur of the moment when they heard his name being read out. McWilliams climbed through a pre-cut hole in a fence and clambered over a roof before making the move. CCTV cameras that were supposed to be monitoring the area were turned off and the control tower looking over the area was unmanned.

After killing Wright, McWilliams made his way back to his cell laughing. He handed over a 9mm Makarov pistol and a double-barrelled .22 Derringer, which had been smuggled into the prison, to a priest before surrendering. He and the other two Provos involved in the attack were given life.

Seen by many as the extremists on either side, neither the LVF nor the INLA was on ceasefire and the authorities claimed that this was the reason they were locked up together. But Wright shouldn't have left Maghaberry in the first place. It was made plain to both sides that, once the peace process started, any paramilitaries caught doing anything illegal would be treated as ordinary criminals. That meant they wouldn't be eligible for any deals. So why was he moved to the Maze?

At the time, a spokesman for the political wing of the INLA warned what was going to happen. He said, 'The transfer of Billy Wright to an INLA H-Block is a serious error of judgement. I just hope the relevant authorities realise this and take corrective action immediately.'

I didn't see him once during the whole time he was in the Maze, because of where he was being held.

Michael Stone told me what had happened. Stone rarely

came on to our wing, so when he did I knew it must be serious. I was lying on my bed when he walked in and told me Wright had been shot. The blood drained from my face. I couldn't believe it. The UVF had shafted him and now the security services had engineered a situation resulting in his death. Most importantly for the whole of Northern Ireland, it almost derailed the whole peace process.

In August 1994, the IRA announced a 'cessation of all military operations'. I remember seeing pictures of the cars driving up the Falls Road with tricolours hanging from the windows and horns being blasted. The Catholic population thought they were on the verge of getting a united Ireland. The ceasefire represented the first stage in getting what they wanted without shooting or using bombs. The whole country breathed a huge sigh of relief because it looked like the guns were going to be put away.

I wasn't happy with the way the IRA had gone about it. They had killed key Loyalists Ray Smallwoods, Joe Bratty and Raymond Elder not just to test the UDA with me off the streets, but also because they wouldn't be able to deal with them around the negotiating table. They had carried out one last bit of dirty work before claiming they wanted peace.

John White, the spokesman for Loyalist prisoners, had co-founded the UFF in 1973 and, more importantly, I trusted him. He came to me and said we had to grab the opportunity for peace while we could. It wasn't going to happen overnight, but slowly good would come from the talks. He had served life for murder and been at the heart of the movement for years. If he said it was the right move to make, I was happy with that and would do everything I could to bring the prisoners with me. From a selfish point of view, I felt a degree of relief to think that the attacks on me might stop.

On the day the IRA ceasefire was announced, Ricky Calderwood and I were lifted out of the Maze and taken to Castlereagh. On the face of it, they told us we were to be questioned about the abduction and beating of a police informant. But when I told them I knew nothing about it they stopped the questioning straight away. The real reason I was there soon became clear. Two senior detectives had been sent down to quiz me and see what I thought about what the IRA were doing.

It would be easy for people like me to ignore what was happening and call for the killing to continue. We had them on the run, after all. It was also easy because prisoners had nothing to lose and we wouldn't be the ones squeezing the trigger or facing the prospect of capture. I made it plain to them that, if it meant there would be no more killing of my people, I was happy to go along with the process and see where it took us.

However, there were prisoners who were desperate to get on board the peace bus because they thought it would secure their release. It was true we would all have to be part of the solution in the end, but it wasn't going to happen overnight. The cons who had been locked up for a while could see the light at the end of the tunnel for the first time and were desperate for the war to be over so they could get home to their families.

Early release was, for many outside, no doubt the hardest pill to swallow of the whole peace process, but it was a risk that needed to be taken for an agreement to be reached. The difficulty was that some of the prisoners thought that, with the IRA ceasefire, the door of the Maze would open up and we would stroll off into the sunset. It was never going to work like that, but the chance of freedom pushed some to the edge. The negotiations took a long time and were about more than just the prisoners. It was on the agenda but nothing was ever concrete. Trying to explain that to the rest of the lads wasn't easy; they wanted out yesterday, and in February 1996 it got much worse.

Disillusioned with the way the peace process negotiations were going, the IRA detonated a massive bomb in a car park close to Canary Wharf in London. Two men were killed, more than 100 injured and there was £85 million worth of damage. When we heard about it in the Maze, we were devastated. The double blow of the IRA going back to bombing and our chances of release disappearing were savage. For 18 months, there had seemed like a chance of peace and in an instant it was gone.

Hatred of the IRA reached new levels because they had stopped the peace bus rolling into the Maze and picking up prisoners. I could see it in the men's faces: they were totally lost and were looking to me for answers. I had none.

In June, the campaign continued with a half-ton bomb that devastated the centre of Manchester, causing £100 million worth of damage and injuring 200 people. It wasn't until July of the following year that the IRA called another ceasefire and the light at the end of the tunnel could be seen again. But, by Christmas 1997, Billy Wright was dead and the peace talks seemed to have swung firmly in favour of the Republicans. This time it was us who were prepared to walk away.

A delegation from the UDP went to London to explain how desperate the situation was after the murder of Wright. They also made it clear that Loyalist prisoners feared the Union was being sold down the river and the Nationalists were getting all the concessions. The chances of a lasting deal were fading fast.

Downing Street agreed something had to be done and Dr Mo Mowlam decided she would come and visit us in the Maze. I'd met her once before in 1996 when she was Shadow Secretary of State. This was different. The Northern Ireland Secretary was putting her political life on the line in an effort to bring us back from the brink.

On 9 January 1998, Sam McCrory, Michael Stone, Bobby Philpott, Glen Cunningham and I had a 50-minute meeting with her. She had no problem being in the same room as us and was relaxed. With her shoes off and snapping her fingers when she wanted a light for a cigarette, Dr Mowlam insisted there was no bias to the Nationalists and both sides were going to have to make tough decisions. It was an exercise in convincing us that pulling out would be a mistake. How would we have any influence over the decisions that were going to be made if our representatives weren't at the talks?

Dr Mowlam asked me directly what would happen if the

Provos killed someone close to me. I answered by saying I hoped that day wouldn't come. Afterwards, she told reporters, 'It wasn't easy. I apologise to those who were offended and thank others who supported me. I have listened and it's a difficult balance, but I don't want to leave any stone unturned. I want to be sure we did everything we could to keep the process moving forward. No concessions and no guarantees were made.'

Despite Mo Mowlam's brave actions, there were those who were furious. Tory MP Nicholas Winterton described her visit as a 'diabolical instance of pandering to terrorism'. But if she hadn't come to the Maze I seriously doubt the Good Friday Agreement would have been signed in April that year.

The early-release process was up and running. Prisoners had to fill in a form detailing why they were locked up and for how long, and submit it to a commission that would decide when they could walk out. At first I got the green light but then I was knocked back when the security services decided I would be a risk to the peace process. For six weeks I sat and sweated, wondering if I was ever going to get out. I was furious about not being freed; it felt like a betrayal. I was about to go and fight my case in front of the commission when Mo Mowlam reversed the decision.

On 14 September 1999, I became the 293rd prisoner to walk out of the Maze. The night before, I got together with the few who were still left on the wing and they presented me with a silver tray bearing an inscription thanking me for all the work I'd done for the prisoners.

Walking out was the hardest thing I did the whole time I was there and my eyes were filled with tears. I was grateful that it was the end for me and I was going back to my family, but it was tough leaving the others behind. As I stood waiting to go through the turnstile and get back to the Shankill, the screws warned me there were hundreds of media and supporters waiting for me to make an appearance.

When I walked out, it hit me in waves. The reporters were shouting questions backed up by the machine-gun fire of the camera shutters. As I raised my head, I recognised faces in the crowd before catching a glimpse of someone else I knew.

My minders grabbed me and got me into the car as quickly as possible. Nothing was going to get in their way. Snappers who were trying to get in close were brushed aside and I was bundled into the back of the car. I'd been warned my life was in danger as soon as I left the prison. I was ducked down in the back of the car with a bulletproof vest over my head as we sped off.

The C Company men who met me had hired three cars of the same colour. If an IRA spotter was in the car park he would note the car I was in and radio it ahead to an ASU waiting down the road. To be absolutely sure, I was also transferred from one car to the other about a mile down the road, in case the licence plate had been taken down as well. No attack came and when I got home the place was overrun with well-wishers and for two days a constant stream of people came to see me. I was given so much cash from my supporters I was able to take the whole family on holiday to Jamaica. Happy days.

14

BACK INSIDE

So much had changed while I was in prison. Now, at the same time that I was able to be with my family again, the peace process was moving forward and slowly the picture in Northern Ireland was beginning to change. It was an incredible time. Just a few years earlier, it would have seemed impossible to say that our struggle would have taken us so far. And yet here we were in negotiations with our sworn enemies and working slowly towards some kind of peace. But that didn't mean I could relax.

From the moment I walked out of the Maze, there were always going to be people who wanted me locked up again or, even better, dead. The security forces and my enemies were watching closely to see what I was going to do. But I was genuinely glad to be part of what was going on and it was clear there was a role for me to play. The commonly held perception was that I hated everything Catholic and, despite what was happening in Northern Ireland, I wouldn't change. It wasn't true and I was advised to try to make an effort to let the Republican community know that.

The first move was to speak with journalists from Catholic areas and get them to write about the way things were. Naturally, this was going to be tough but I was willing to give it a go. A reporter from the *North Belfast News* was asked if he would like to interview me. I remember meeting him close to the peace line and when he got out of the car he was shaking like a leaf. He looked like he thought I was going to take him back to the Shankill and eat him.

I wanted people to know I was sincere about peace. I was constantly being asked to do interviews for the media and in these I tried to answer my critics' claims about what I was up to.

On 29 July 2000, in a chat with the *Independent*, I said what I thought about the rumours going around that I was to be returned to jail. I told the reporter, 'I do not believe the Loyalist community will tolerate my removal. If that happens there will be a reaction and the peace process would be in danger. I'm fighting to keep the peace process but others want to see me eliminated. The UVF want me six feet under and so do figures in authority. I know I'm a target and I have to spend the rest of my life looking over my shoulder. I've spent my time since I was released keeping this peace process going. They said I was a murdering bastard, now they say I'm a drug dealer and I'm involved in terrorism. The RUC Chief Constable says he is having me kept under special observation. So where's the evidence of all my crimes?

'I'm not building up an alliance with the LVF and I do not want a civil war among Loyalists. But I have friends in the LVF who I'm not prepared to abandon. There has been a lot of hurt and a lot of pain. It is a pity it has taken 30 years and 3,000 lives to get this peace process.' I was determined the message was going to be clear. I wasn't looking for trouble.

There were also those in the corporate world who weren't happy about my increasing public profile. A representative from Nike called me and asked if I would stop wearing their clothes and someone even called from Tina Turner's record label and demanded I stop using 'Simply the Best' as a theme tune for the UDA. As far as I was concerned, they should have been paying me for endorsing their products.

It wasn't long until I bumped into a few of my old enemies. I clocked Republican militant Eddie Copeland driving out of the Shankill and back towards the Ardoyne. It may have been peacetime but I still wanted to know what he had been up to. I tugged hard at the steering wheel and sped after him to see what he was doing sniffing about on our patch. Copeland hadn't noticed I was on his tail but was still calm when I confronted him outside his home. Gina was in the car with me, so he knew there wasn't much chance of things getting out of hand.

To begin with, it was a bit of nervous banter, testing each other out to see the lie of the land now that I'd been released. It didn't take long for the mood to change. 'Ah,

Johnny,' Copeland started, 'you're some size now, with the body-building. I see you have some fancy security on your new place.'

While I was locked up, Gina had moved to a new house 50 yards from the peace line. C Company's security boys weren't happy I was living so close to the staunchest of Republican strongholds but it didn't bother me. I looked at him and held his stare. 'Eddie, don't kick sleeping dogs,' I warned, 'because they'll turn round and bite you.'

The IRA had murdered one of the gang who beat me up when I was shot in the head from point-blank range at a UB40 gig. Ed 'Crispy' McCoy was one of Belfast's biggest drug dealers and was gunned down as he sipped a pint in a city bar. The Provos had run him out of the city but after a while he made the mistake of coming back. In May 2000, he was shot in the Motte and Bailey Bar and died 12 hours later.

Republicans did have a go at me on the second anniversary of the Omagh bomb. In August 1998 the Real IRA detonated a 500-pound bomb in the centre of the town in County Tyrone, killing 29 people. Two years on, Nationalists tried to murder me but I don't think there was any significance in the timing of the attempt; it was more down to luck that they got their chance. I was parking my car on the Protestant side of the peace line when a car pulled up alongside me and a blast bomb was thrown on to the bonnet. The explosion shattered the windscreen and showered me with shards of glass.

Later, they tried to claim it was nothing to do with them because the IRA didn't use that sort of device. But that was exactly the point. They were on ceasefire and if any explosive or gun attack was traced back to them the consequences would be dire. In the end, though, it wasn't the IRA who caused me the biggest problems, but some in the Loyalist movement.

A Loyalist community festival was set up for August and was in the planning for months. What started off as one of the best days of my life was soon to become one of the worst.

Thousands of people turned up to enjoy themselves, not just paramilitary figures but also ordinary members of the community from all over Northern Ireland. There was a parade and I walked at the head of it down the Shankill and past the people who lined the streets clapping and cheering. I felt immensely proud to be involved and that the public were showing me their appreciation. But after about 20 minutes the parade descended into chaos.

A Loyalist flute band from Antrim unfurled a flag of the LVF as they began their march. As they marched past the Rex Bar, a well-known UVF haunt, things turned nasty. Their feud with the LVF was still festering away.

That year Richard Jameson of the UVF, Andrew Robb and David McIlwaine had all been murdered in tit-for-tat attacks. A UVF guy called Winkie decided he wasn't going to accept the banner. He stumbled up to the flag carrier and attempted to smash a pint glass in his face. A mass brawl soon broke out.

I was about a mile away talking to people at the side of

the stage that had been erected. Throughout the day, prominent Loyalists took to the stage and gave speeches. Michael Stone and I got up and accepted the applause of the people, which was followed by a group of masked men coming on and firing a volley of shots from AK-47s into the sky. But the mood had changed. Word was coming through about what was going on at the Rex. A drunken mob of UDA men decided to take things into their own hands and headed for the bar.

The UVF troublemakers realised what was coming and barricaded themselves in. Guns were produced and shots were fired, leaving several people injured, including a woman. Within minutes, the situation got totally out of hand. The Shankill was almost entirely UDA, but there were members of the UVF who had lived there all their lives. They were blamed for what had happened at the Rex and were targeted for revenge. The result was mayhem.

Fuelled by drink, youngsters from the Shankill attacked UVF houses with petrol bombs in an attempt to force them out. The UVF should have waited until the Monday morning and gone through the proper channels to make a complaint, not attack the guy in the street. If Winkie had stood there and let the parade pass, nobody would have lost their life. I tried to calm the situation and made an effort to stop things getting out of hand. If the UVF were looking for trouble, I would take them on, but I didn't want people forced out of their homes. Within hours, the community was ripped apart.

A second gun attack was carried out on the Rex Bar and

shots were again fired, this time leaving two people injured. The police had to be brought in to try to keep the two sides apart. It would never be the same again, and there was only one person who was going to get the blame for what had happened: me.

Two days after the trouble flared up, the UVF killed Jackie Coulter and Bobby Mahood. They were sitting in a 4x4 when a gunman walked up and opened fire into the vehicle. Coulter, a member of the UDA, died at the scene. Mahood, who had connections with the UVF, died a short time later in the Mater Hospital. An office used by the UDA Prisoners' Association was bombed that same night. The violence spiralled further as all bus services were stopped and the RUC called for the army to be deployed again on the streets of Belfast.

Jackie Coulter had been a friend of mine and the security services were determined that there shouldn't be another surge in violence. I'd been tipped off that Peter Mandelson, who had taken over from Mo Mowlam as Northern Ireland Secretary the previous October, was going to have my licence revoked. At this stage, nobody released under the Good Friday Agreement had been taken off the streets and locked up again, so I wasn't too convinced it was going to happen. But the plan was given the go-ahead on 22 August.

I was in my car when I was pulled over by a police patrol outside the leisure centre. The copper was fine and I didn't for a moment see what was about to happen. I got out from behind the wheel and stepped to the roadside. As the two of us chatted away, out of the corner of my eye I noticed an army personnel vehicle reversing out on to the road. Before I knew what was going on they were on top of me.

A large door swung open to reveal a SWAT team dressed from head to toe in black and armed to the teeth. They spilled out, each with one arm thrusting forward holding a large transparent Perspex shield. I'd seen a riot squad in action before but nothing like this. For a split second I was sure I was going to be killed there and then. The team of men threw me to the floor and pinned me down using the shields. My head was jammed between the tarmac and the full weight of an officer as the others yanked my arms behind my back and secured me in cuffs. I was then hauled to my feet and marched to the back of the APC before being thrown inside. As I lay on the floor, one of the officers thrust a bit of paper in front of me and told me my licence had been revoked. It was a massive relief. I was going back to prison and not being taken away to be killed.

As the vehicle moved off, none of the hooded soldiers uttered a word. I could just see out of the front window and tried to get a clue where I was being taken. After a short journey, I recognised the security gates of the Girdwood army barracks, where I'd attended a cadet training camp as a child. Within moments we had come to a sudden stop next to a football pitch. My heart pounded as I sat waiting for what was going to happen next.

The commander of the unit started communicating to the others with hand signals, causing my paranoia to come flooding back. Then he turned to me, eyes fixed, and said,

'When you get out you will feel a big suction. Don't worry about it, just keep your head down.'

That was all the explanation I got. The doors were opened and I was bundled out on to the grass, where a Wessex helicopter was waiting. The thud of the rotating blades and the pressure of the draft buffeted me as I was hustled to the open door. Once I was loaded into the back and strapped into my seat a hooded figure sat on one side of me and another two opposite. I'd never been in a helicopter before and fear was clearly written all over my face because one of the troops sniggered and asked if I was frightened.

The door was left open and as we took off my panic deepened. I scanned the interior desperately and when I looked up I fixed my eyes on the back of the pilot's legs, on his combats and shiny boots. Our flight took us back over the Shankill and to within a couple of hundred yards of my house. Only a few minutes earlier, I'd been safe at home. Now I was watching from a chopper as more security services on the ground set about smashing down my front door. Word had spread quickly about my being snatched off the street and Gina managed to get the steel shutters down. I caught a glimpse of the cops brawling in the street with C Company men as they tried to get into my house

The entire operation to deliver me to Maghaberry Prison took minutes. The Maze was no more and I was in with ordinary cons. The first night I lay in the cell furious I was back inside and wondering how they were going to deal with me. If I hadn't been recalled, there was every chance I would have used my influence to calm the situation, not make it worse.

Mandelson said in a statement, 'I took the decision to suspend the licence of this prisoner after receiving a full report from the security forces and on the advice of the police. My priority is public safety and I cannot give freedom to an individual intent on abusing it. I am satisfied that this particular individual had breached the terms of his licence. I won't allow anyone to prejudice the interests of the whole community. The people of Belfast do not want to live under the heel of gangsters and thugs who use old-style paramilitary methods for their own end.'

It was clear who he thought was to blame for what was going on. After a night in my cell I was brought in front of the governor and the head of security. They were nervous about how I was going to react. The prison held both Protestants and Catholics and the two officials tried to convince me that for this reason they couldn't guarantee my safety. In other words, they wanted to throw me into isolation and forget about me. But I wasn't having that. They had revoked my licence and I was entitled to go on to the wings with the rest of them. It wasn't long before I settled back into prison life and got on with the time I was going to have to do.

I did make an effort to overturn Mandelson's ruling and at first the sentence review commission agreed I'd been unfairly recalled. But then the big guns were turned on me to ensure I wasn't getting out. During a two-day hearing in the prison, Sir Ronnie Flanagan, Chief Constable of the

RUC, and two of the most senior Special Branch officers in the country gave what they said was a detailed account of what I'd been up to since being freed from the Maze.

They were getting intelligence not just from officers in the field but also from touts on the inside of the UDA who would have been delighted to have seen me off the streets. Unfortunately, my lawyer and I weren't allowed to see the evidence, so we had no chance to prepare any sort of defence. What Flanagan and Special Branch were doing was effectively legalised internment. Who were the commission going to believe? The chief constable or someone just released from a 16-year stretch? So I remained inside.

On the surface, the prisoners inside Maghaberry were able to tolerate one another, but tensions lurked underneath. A core of INLA men more or less ran the place and strutted about in Celtic shirts keeping the Protestants in their place. I didn't know many people there and naturally the Catholics didn't want to have anything to do with me. If I walked into the canteen and I was the only Protestant, I would be greeted by hard stares and a wall of silence.

There was always trouble in the exercise yard when the INLA played football. The young Protestants would get lumps kicked out of them and they would just take it. Something had to be done. Danny Hughes was the top INLA man. What he said went and most people in Maghaberry feared him. If the trouble was going to stop, he was the man to make it happen.

I strode up to his cell with nobody to back me up and

clocked him loitering about surrounded by his men. As I got closer, a couple of them puffed their chests out to make it clear they were ready for any trouble. I got to Hughes and told him I was going to hold him personally responsible if there was any more trouble for the Protestants in the prison. It wasn't a deal that could be negotiated. Before any trouble could flare up, the wardens moved in and locked us down for the night.

The next morning I was in the shower when Hughes and a couple of his men came in. I was on my own again, so I thought there was a chance my warning was about to be thrown back in my face. Hughes came up to me, stretched out his hand and said we had a deal as long as I spoke to the troublemakers on my side. I think he respected me for coming on to his landing with no back-up and having a word with him.

The amount of trouble decreased. Being in Maghaberry became like being back in Crumlin Road Opportunities. I was in the company of Catholics almost 24 hours a day, which, as a brigadier in the UDA, didn't happen often. The longer I was there, the more I realised I could get along with them without any trouble at all.

While I was inside, Stevie McKeag was found dead in his flat. Winkie Dodds and Donald Hodgen had taken over the running of C Company and, without me to keep a tight rein on Stevie, he was allowed to run riot. To make matters worse, he had been in a motorbike accident after which he was never the same. The smash had left him dependent on painkillers and he was taking massive amounts of cocaine. Paranoia soon got a grip of him and he became a virtual recluse.

An inquest heard how he smashed up his house on the night he died and a crossbow bolt had been fired. Some people claimed that I'd somehow managed to have him killed but that was total nonsense. Sadly, it was a drugs overdose that killed him. Things were far from perfect with Stevie before he died but it was still a tough blow to take when I heard he was gone. Being locked up and unable to make a difference is the hardest thing about prison, especially when something like that happens. I just had to get on with doing my time.

Maghaberry wasn't like the Maze, but there were things that I had to deal with. A Real IRA remand prisoner was brought in and soon became the talk of the place. Rumours were flying about he was an unhinged psycho who was going to terrorise the whole jail. He'd been caught with a sniper's rifle and had done time in the Maze.

For several months, his reputation grew and grew to the point where I wanted to see what all the fuss was about. Days after he was sentenced and moved from the remand cells into the main part of the jail, I came across him in the canteen. I threw him a dirty look and he didn't react, but it wasn't long until it did kick off. There was a fight and a pal of mine got his head caved in with a clothes iron by two Catholics. I immediately assumed the Real IRA man was behind the attack, but there was nothing I could do that night as the screws locked us down.

First thing the following morning, I went to see him.

Relations between the factions had deteriorated since he'd come on the scene. Most of us had just wanted to get on with doing our time until he turned up. When I got on to his landing, he was outside emptying his rubbish and as I got nearer to him I told him to go back inside the cell. I followed him in expecting the two of us to get stuck into each other but when I strode in I couldn't believe my eyes. He was crouched in a ball leaning against the wall trying to protect himself and whimpering, 'It was nothing to do with me, Johnny. Honest, it really wasn't.'

I didn't know what to do. I was hyped and ready to go toe to toe with this notorious Real IRA man, who was now begging for mercy. Instead of fighting, I listened to him and in the end believed he really hadn't ordered the attack. The two of us came to an agreement that if there was any trouble we would meet and discuss what had to be done. As time went on, we respected each other and even swapped books. There was an amicable arrangement that we would both just try to do our time in peace.

I still faced a concerted effort by my enemies to do what they could to discredit me and the best way to do that was to give the newspapers stories about me. For a couple of months, the red-top tabloids kept running exclusives claiming I was running a vice ring from behind bars. It drove me nuts. C Company pulled in a lot of cash but none of it came from hookers. Then, one of the inmates let something slip during a visit. That day, another prostitution tale had appeared and I was moaning to him about it. Sheepishly, he admitted he and a couple of others had been lifting cash from a brothel for months. When things were getting slow, they were showing a picture of me to the girls and telling them if they didn't get more punters in I was going to come and get them when I got out. I was furious. I was trying to convince the authorities I wasn't a threat and should be let out and they were running hookers in my name.

Maghaberry still had smuggling operations going on, although not as big as those in the Maze had been. As in every jail in the UK, all sorts of things were valuable to cons. I had a pal that I used to go and hang about with when I could. He was in debt to me and in turn a Catholic he knew owed him a few favours. Normally I would get phone cards from him to settle the debt but his pal could get protein drinks in. I was still heavily into weight training, so I asked if he could get me some protein-rich powder mix to help me gain weight and train.

For weeks, the arrangement worked fine with no problems. Eventually, the Catholic realised there was an opportunity staring him in the face. My mate was a tall skinny guy and there was no way he was taking the protein drink. INLA hoods worked this out and had strychnine smuggled on to the wing. It was added to the powder by making a very small slice in the silver seal.

Three times a day, I would make a milk shake with the mixture, leave it in my cell and drink it whenever I wanted to. The night I was poisoned I'd been on a visit and returned to my cell before being locked up for the night. I grabbed the shake that was already mixed up and took a swig. The moment it hit my tongue I knew something was wrong. It was like an electric shock stinging my mouth. Straight away I spat it out.

My first thought was that the milk must have been off, yet it hadn't been there very long. I shook off the feeling, sat down on the bed and started to read the papers when I started to go really strange. It was as if I'd been spiked with an acid tab. I checked my pupils in the mirror and they were fine. After a couple of hours, the sensation went away and I got to sleep.

The next morning I went to see my pal who had got the stuff for me and asked him if he knew anything about it. After denying he had spiked me, he had a tiny taste of what was left and agreed it was rank. The only thing left to do was to get the screws involved. To begin with, I was reluctant but my pal was insistent something wasn't right.

The prison staff were anxious to keep everything under wraps and I was taken to see the doctor when the rest of the cons were locked up. I explained what had happened and he took away the drink to test what was in it. A few days later, I was sent for again during lockdown to be told the results.

The moment I walked into the room, I could see something was wrong. Prison security bosses were there as well as the doctor. He started by telling me that strychnine had been discovered in the shake and then explained what it was. If I'd drunk a large amount of the mix, I would have died a slow death locked in my cell. They knew I was furious and was likely to be hell-bent on revenge, so they tried to convince me that for my own safety it would be better if I was moved.

I knew it would have been Catholics who had tried to poison me but I had no idea how they managed to pull it off. The screws checked CCTV footage and ruled out the possibility that someone had gone into the cell and contaminated it while I was out. Almost a year later, I found out the truth.

It was Christmas time and a Catholic lad full of ecstasy was partying with a few of my associates when he revealed how the plot was carried out. If he hadn't told them the INLA were behind it, I doubt I would have ever known. By that stage, I was almost ready for release, having served half of my original sentence, and had been moved to a different part of the prison. There was no point in causing myself trouble so close to walking out of the prison gates.

15

AN ANCIENT FEUD

I'd tasted freedom before and had it snatched away from me. I'd faced danger inside and a slow agonising death by poison while locked up. But still they hadn't managed to take me out. And the peace process was still ongoing as well. As I prepared for life outside of prison again, I knew there was still everything to play for.

When I walked out of Maghaberry in May 2002, the Inner Council faces were all there as a show of UDA unity. In turn, Jim Gray, Billy 'The Mexican' McFarland, Jimbo 'Bacardi Brigadier' Simpson, John 'Grugg' Gregg and Jackie McDonald welcomed me back in front of the television cameras.

Three hundred people cheered wildly and fireworks were let off as John White told the waiting reporters, 'The nationalist community need not fear his release. Johnny

Adair will be a force for good in this province. He will continue to make a positive contribution to the peace process and endeavour to help bring solutions to problems in many parts of the community.' It was the message we wanted to get across and it was genuine.

C Company security took me back to the Shankill, where a party was waiting for me. Along the way we were accompanied by a convoy of cars waving Union flags and a banner with 'Welcome Home Johnny' plastered across it greeted me at the estate. Friends and family toasted my release with bottles of champagne carrying labels that read 'C Company Johnny Mad Dog Adair 15 May 2002' to commemorate the occasion.

The security services had hoped my return would be a quiet one and vowed I would be kept under round-the-clock surveillance. They were desperate to keep me locked up and within eight months they were to get what they wanted, with the added bonus of the implosion of the UDA.

The previous Loyalist feud had been sorted out while I was in Maghaberry, but only after a spate of tit-for-tat killings claimed the lives of Samuel Rocket, David Greer, Bertie Rice, Tommy English and Mark Quail. Hundreds of people were evicted from their homes as both the UDA and UVF cleansed their territory of anyone they thought was the enemy.

The causes of the feuds went back a long way. Both factions of the Loyalist paramilitaries had always held grudges against each other but forgot them and united against the common enemy of the Republican movement.

Now, though, the IRA guns were silent and it was far easier for the old jealousies to return.

Everything was still fine in July, when I met the Northern Ireland Secretary, Dr John Reid, at the East Belfast Mission Hall as part of the Loyalist Commission. Sectarian tensions had been rising since the Holy Cross Primary School 12-week picket in June the previous year, which I'd helped to bring to an end. Dr Reid insisted we all had to work together to stop the violence and, as before, I wanted to do what I could.

One problem that was dealt with was my son Jonathan, whose anti-social behaviour was bringing him to the attention of the UDA. As a kid, he was a very promising footballer and that was all he was really interested in. But when he hit 15 he lost interest and with me locked up he started getting himself into trouble. Our house on Manor Street was right on the peace line between Catholics and Protestants and it wasn't long until he was involved in sectarian clashes. The first time I had any idea was when the cops came to the house and invited Gina to the police station to look at some CCTV footage of him fighting with Catholic kids. I honestly thought he was a quiet lad and wasn't interested in going down the same road as me.

The last thing I wanted for him was thinking he had to live up to my reputation. The people around him were more likely to refer to him as Johnny Adair's son and not Jonathan. It was almost expected he would be another version of me but I didn't want that.

Most of the time he kept out of the way of the cops but

he did have run-ins with the paramilitaries who ran the community. The crowd he was hanging about with were into joyriding old cars with no driving licence or insurance. Anti-social behaviour like that was bound to get him into trouble.

The UDA were pulling him and his pals regularly and warning them to get a grip. There was only so many times I could plead his case and say the situation was going to be sorted out. Then he was shot in the leg.

The first I knew about it was when someone turned up at my door and told me. The papers picked up on it straight away and the line was that I'd ordered him shot. There was no way I would be involved in anything like that. Had I been able to stop it, of course I would have. I went to the hospital to see my son and get his side of the story but he wouldn't tell me anything other than that it was anti-social behaviour. Belfast is a vicious place and this sort of thing is commonplace. You weren't going to get fined £30 if you stepped out of line; you would face more serious consequences. Most members of the public would rather go to the paramilitaries if they wanted something done than speak to the cops. What Jonathan got was minor and nothing more than a warning. Other lads were kneecapped or had their elbows blown out. I remember a kid caught joyriding was nailed to a fence. When the emergency team came to take him to the hospital, they had to cut him down.

Even with Jonathan having been punished, there were still major obstacles to overcome and, as it turned out, any hope of a lasting truce within the UDA was destroyed with the murder of Stephen Warnock. I was standing in the square outside my house when I got a call to let me know what had happened.

Stephen was shot 15 times by a motorbike passenger as he sat in his BMW in Newtownards in County Down with his three-year-old daughter in the back. The police said the gunmen couldn't have failed to see the child and described the act as 'despicable'. Stephen was a friend of mine and I was shocked about what had happened. The first thing I did was go to the family's house to pay my respects. They had been through plenty before. Two of Stephen's brothers had been killed in 1972. Robert was shot dead by an off-duty policeman during an attempted robbery and William was knocked down and killed by an army vehicle at just 15. But this devastated the family.

Although Stephen was an LVF man, it was unlikely the shooting was anything to do with the Provos as it was peacetime. While I was visiting the Warnocks, I was asked into a side room by one of Stephen's brothers. The tears were streaming down his face. He looked me in the eye and asked if I'd sanctioned the murder. I had no idea what he was going on about and had assumed the UVF were behind the hit. It was certainly nothing to do with me. He asked me again, did I give the go-ahead? I insisted I knew nothing about it.

The gunmen dumped their motorbike in east Belfast and Stephen's brother had intelligence suggesting the UDA commander of the area, Jim Gray, ordered the killing. There was a taped conversation that seemed to confirm what was being alleged. If Gray had called for the hit, Stephen's family thought I'd given the OK for it to be done. That meant I was in a house full of LVF men out for revenge who thought I was behind the murder of their comrade.

I managed to get them to believe I had nothing to do with it and suggested we try to get hold of Gray to hear his side of the story. Through our political people, he was told he was getting the blame for what had happened and should come forward and explain. Gray wasn't prepared to meet, which right away made him look guilty. If I was accused of something I had nothing to do with, I would make sure everyone knew I was innocent. Gray didn't and effectively put his head in the noose. For days and days, he stayed out of the way, only serving to fuel speculation and anger. A witness then came forward and told the Inner Council compelling evidence that put Gray in the frame. They believed the account and the pressure on him continued to grow.

Stephen Warnock's murder had echoes of the Mafia-style killing of Geordie Legge in January 2001. The 37-year-old's body was found with multiple stab wounds in the back and his throat had been cut. Gray was widely thought to have been involved. He owned the Bunch of Grapes pub, where Legge was murdered, and was one of five men questioned by the police. The killers disposed of the body by rolling it up in a carpet from the pub and also set the building on fire.

Legge's mother, Margaret, told the coroner's court she blamed Gray for the killing, saying, 'I know they had a few rows. I heard him threatening to burn us out of the flat.'

The police described the murder as one of the worst since

the reign of the Shankill Butchers during the 1970s. Gray was looking increasingly like he wanted to be some sort of Mafia figure who had nobody to answer to. Now Stephen had been disposed of in a similarly callous way.

A close associate of Gray, Frankie Gallagher, turned up at Stephen's wake while I was there. Gallagher reported back to Gray that I'd been in the Warnocks' house. Gray realised it was time for him to show his face and went there to pay his respects.

As he left to go home and was about to get into his BMW, he turned round to see a gunman standing at point-blank range in front of him. He was shot in the face. The bullet shattered his jawbone and teeth before exiting on the other side. Had he not turned his head when he heard the gunman approach, he would have died instantly. Instead, he was able to stagger away and get help before being taken to hospital.

Because I had friends among the LVF, I got the blame for the attempt on Gray. One fairytale even placed me at the scene, watching from a nearby building. I had no sympathy for Gray as he was the man suspected of killing Stephen. But it wasn't up to me to tell the LVF what to do and I was on the Shankill at the time of the attack.

Gray's shooting infuriated the Inner Council and I was ordered not to go to Stephen's funeral as the gunman would likely be there. But there was no way I was going to turn my back on the Warnock family. My defiance proved too much for the Inner Council. Days later, a statement was released by the UDA saying, 'As a result of ongoing investigations, the present Brigadier of West Belfast is no longer accepted in our organisation.'

When reporters came and asked me what I thought about the statement, I told them it wasn't worth the paper it was written on, ripped it up and suggested they ask the UDA what it was about.

Within hours, a banner went up on the Shankill declaring, 'West Belfast Brigade – business as usual, no change.'

From there, the split worsened and the violence escalated. A bomb was found outside John White's home in Carrickfergus and two days after that a device was discovered under the car of John 'Grugg' Gregg, the UDA's brigadier of south-east Antrim.

Gregg, who was jailed after an assassination attempt on Gerry Adams in 1984, now decided I had to be killed at all costs. Two gunmen, Henry Smith and Daryl Coulter, were sent to kill me as I dropped 11-year-old Chloe off at school. The pair of them were caught as, armed with an automatic pistol, they made their way across Belfast on a motorbike. The police warned me there was a plan to kill me at the school and suggested I stay away. But I wasn't going to let threats keep me a prisoner in my own home. The cops clearly had accurate intelligence and were on top of the situation, so I was happy to put my faith in them.

After Smith and Coulter were caught, the UDA leadership tried to claim they were from the Red Hand Defenders and were on their way to kill a top Republican in the Ardoyne. The truth of it was that now the plan had failed they were frightened I might realise what they were up to and go after them.

Instead, intermediaries were sent to Gregg on behalf of C Company to offer a truce and affirm that there was no need for the violence. It was made clear that action would be taken if provoked. Gregg wasn't interested.

On Boxing Day, Jonathan Stewart was shot in the kitchen of a house on Manor Street, where he was attending a party. The 22-year-old was the nephew of Alan McClean, a former C Company man who had sided with the UDA. An associate of mine, Ian Truesdale, whose daughter had been going out with Stewart, was arrested and held on remand for the murder for six months before the charge was dropped. Ian was stuck in the frame by his brother, who had become a police informant and fed them total nonsense. It has been claimed I had Stewart killed because his uncle stole from C Company and then switched sides. The lad was an entirely innocent victim and what happened to him was a disgrace. Stewart shouldn't have been caught up in it.

Just over a week later, the feud claimed another victim when Roy Green was shot dead as he left the Kimberley Bar. After the hit, the UDA issued a statement which said, 'We regret the grief and sadness visited upon the Green family, but treason is treason. Our enquiries reveal that Green had been acting as a double agent between C Company and members of the North and South Belfast UFF.

'Green declared on many occasions that, whilst Adair was a friend of his, he thought that Adair and John White should die for their actions against the organisation and he revealed he had plans to set Adair up for execution.'

Although a dedicated member of the UFF and active during the Troubles, Green had nothing to do with the feuds. However, the fact he kept visiting me was enough to sign his death warrant. On the day of his funeral, Gregg sent another team to try to kill me. I was lying in bed with Gina – the kids weren't in the house because of the ongoing trouble – when I heard a bang. I got up, wandered over to the window and saw what was left of a pipe bomb that had been lobbed at the house. I closed the curtain and went back to bed.

The violence over the festive period was too much for the security services to take and on 10 January the new Northern Ireland Secretary, Paul Murphy, sent the cops round to have me lifted again. He told the press, 'I am satisfied Adair is a danger to others and while he is at liberty is likely to commit further offences.'

The UDA were trying to have me killed but I was the one who had to be taken off the streets. It was easier and less hassle than beginning a whole new investigation. I was out on licence and all they had to do was revoke it.

When I was first jailed in 1995, I expected to do two-thirds of the 16-year sentence. Under the Tony Blair government, it was first reduced to half the original tariff and then further by the Good Friday Agreement. When I was recalled and sent to Maghaberry the first time, it went back up to eight years. On the second recall, the sentence went back up to two-thirds. In the history of the Troubles in Northern Ireland, I was the only prisoner that this happened to.

Murphy had me off the streets and he hoped peace would break out among the warring Loyalist factions. But he wasn't going to take any chances. He wanted me out of the way. While I'd started off on the normal wing of Maghaberry with the rest of the cons and was happy to stay there, during lock-up one night they came to get me. I was 'Rule 32'd' and told I could walk to the isolation wing or they would carry me. It was the usual excuse: I had to be moved for my own safety and for the safety of the other prisoners.

The fact was, the authorities just wanted me in isolation, where I couldn't influence anything. No matter who I complained to, it wasn't going to make any difference, because the order had come from on high. I was to be held on a wing of my own.

It was an eerie part of the prison and it was going to be tough to get my head round. The wing, which was part of the female part of the prison, had been out of use for some time and, although it was clean, there was a layer of dust over everything. It was also where my friend Mark 'Swinger' Fulton had taken his own life by strangling himself with his belt. Seven months earlier, I'd shouldered his coffin as he was laid to rest in Seago Cemetery in County Armagh. Swinger was an LVF man and we had become friends after the death of Billy Wright. Nobody around him had any idea he was suicidal and it was a terrible blow. I could feel Mark all about the wing and I was constantly thinking about him. I wasn't frightened but it made me numb being there on my own with just the memory of what had happened.

In the early days in isolation, there were moments when I wondered how I was going to make it through. Rab 'Rocket Man' Bradshaw had also taken his own life in the main part of the prison after getting his head messed up by a girl. Now I was looking at two years on my own with just a couple of prison guards out on the landing for company. It was bleak. After my previous experience of the sentence review commission, I didn't even bother going to them but resigned myself to the isolation.

I had a double cell on the wing with bunk beds while all the other cell doors were locked. The authorities gave me what everyone else was entitled to, including a pool table with nobody to play with. The place was deathly silent and I have no doubt they were trying to mess with my head. It might not have been their plan to have me kill myself but they wouldn't have complained. The security forces didn't want me complicating the feud in any way and I didn't.

On 1 February 2003, a terrifying blow was dealt to the UDA Inner Council. John 'Grugg' Gregg was murdered. His taxi was riddled with bullets as it pulled up at traffic lights shortly after picking him up from the Stena high-speed ferry, which he had boarded at Stranraer. He and his pal Robert Carson, 33, were making their way back from Glasgow, where they had watched Rangers play Aberdeen at Ibrox Park. Grugg died instantly when a bullet entered his brain and Carson was also killed at the scene.

The first I knew about what had happened was when I

heard the news on the radio in my cell. I feared it was John White who had been killed. The initial reports said that a leading Loyalist had been shot dead in a red car while driving through Belfast docks. I knew John had been away visiting his kids that night and his route back would have gone through the area where the incident happened. He was also running about in my red car. I had to sweat it out for the night before I found out 'Grugg' was the victim. Straight away I was blamed for the hit.

Grugg had been the biggest aggressor during the feud and made numerous efforts to have me and my supporters killed. Did I have him murdered? No. Did I know about it before the operation was carried out? No. Do I regret what happened to him? Absolutely not. Grugg played with fire and got burned.

For the rest it was a war of words, but for him violence was the only way of getting a solution. Grugg saw only himself as the victim and conveniently forgot he was the one who started it all with the bomb left at John White's house. He had issued a statement saying there were five graves waiting to be filled by members of C Company and then sent two gunmen to kill me as I dropped my daughter off at school. When that failed, he tried to blow me up as I slept in my bed. The sad thing is none of it had to happen but he ended up out of his depth.

I knew nothing about the murder and if I had a hand in it the cops would have been all over me. They monitored my phone calls from the isolation block and my visits, and I'm sure they would have known if I'd planned it. With

Grugg dead, the UDA leadership were in turmoil, wondering who was going to be next.

It turned out that Jim Gray was in the clear over the murder of Stephen Warnock. In May 2003, Jim Johnston was gunned down outside his £500,000 house near the village of Crawfordsburn in County Down. The millionaire, who was under investigation by the Assists Recovery Agency, was a member of the Red Hand Commando and blamed for Stephen's death. Johnston was one of the biggest drug barons in Northern Ireland and Special Branch had warned him his life was in danger. After shooting him several times, the gunmen escaped on foot through the fields next to the isolated house.

But it was only a matter of time before Gray got his comeuppance. In March 2005, he was expelled from the UDA and a week later he was stopped by the police trying to flee the country with a bank draft for 10,000 and £3,000 in cash in his car. Seven months later, he was murdered as he got out of his car at his father's home. He was under strict bail conditions which included a curfew and an order insisting he report to the police five times a week. He had become a liability to the UDA and they didn't want him appearing in any court. It was his best mate who lured him to his death.

16

EXILES

I'd been recalled to prison before, but as I sat in isolation I had nothing else to occupy me but the extreme danger of the situation. And more than ever the frustration of not being able to do anything weighed upon me. It was even worse for the people I knew on the outside.

While I was locked up, the UDA knew that revenge on the Shankill for John Gregg's murder would be easy. On the eve of his funeral, they moved to extinguish what was left of C Company. Radio Ulster woke me up at 7am with the news my family and anyone associated with me had been forced from their homes. I'd been given no warning about what was about to happen. My mind was racing. They had all been evicted, but what did that mean?

I paced up and down in my cell for an hour waiting for it to be unlocked before I could get on the phone and try to find out the latest. The moment the door opened, I called Gina's mobile. Chloe answered. Sobbing, she said, 'Daddy, we're in Scotland and the police have us. C Company have run and left us all.'

After trying to reassure them everything would be OK, I rang one of our leaders to see what he knew. He was still in bed. Although he had an idea what was going on, he came up with a load of feeble excuses and told me to call back at lunchtime. When I did, he'd changed his number. He had no reason to stab me in the back but he'd been made an offer he couldn't refuse by the intelligence services

The place on Manor Street was deemed to be too close to the Republican area so we moved to Boundary Way before even a year had passed. My new house was kitted out with state-of-the-art security devices as well as steel shutters and bulletproof glass. Donald Hodgen had bolted for my house the moment the scores of UDA men came to put them out. My former head of security was now only out to protect himself. He was running about daft, crying his eyes out, trying to come up with a plan to save his own neck.

The mob weren't getting into the house. Missiles were being hurled at the windows but it wasn't making any difference. Gina was trying to phone the cops to come down and sort the situation out when Hodgen grabbed the phone from her hand.

My kids were hysterical but he threw them out of the way and got up into the loft. Gina was asking him to calm down and stay where he was. It was pointless: his bottle was gone. Hodgen was panicking so much that when he got into the loft he kept putting his feet through the ceiling of the room below as he searched for any escape route. He was over 20 stone and supposed to be head of security, but the first chance he got Hodgen legged it, leaving women and kids to fend for themselves. The moment the cops turned up, he opened the shutter and bolted. He hasn't been seen since. Before he went to ground, he went to all the stashes of C Company cash and lifted the lot. In all, he got not far off £200,000, £25,000 of which he gave to the UDA to buy his family a bit of time.

When Gina saw Hodgen's reaction and found out that Jackie Thompson and James 'Sham' Millar had led the charge to the boat to Scotland, she was left with little choice but to follow.

Thompson had appointed himself west Belfast brigadier and Hodgen was supposed to be his number two. When it came to the crunch, it was the C Company foot soldiers who stood their ground and fought, not the cowards at the top.

Sitting in my cell, all I could do was watch my family's eviction unfold on the news. I was numb as pictures came in of the removal vans turning up and emptying the furniture out of the house. The cops organised it for all the people who were worried the properties would be looted. In the chaos, my dogs had to be left behind as well. When the UDA found out a neighbour had been kind enough to look after them, they planned to kill them, but the cops got wind of it and stepped in.

With C Company swept aside, the UDA went round trying to mop up cash, weapons and anything else they thought might be useful for them. Anyone who had links to C Company in any way was now grilled and asked if they knew where the stuff was hidden. Gina's 72-year-old mother had her house broken into and a car with a pipe bomb was left outside the front door. She soon followed the rest to the mainland. My brother had his car set on fire twice and when they couldn't get into his house they fired shots through a window. He left as well. The UDA realised what they had done to me and my family and were terrified of any backlash. They pulled out all the stops to find any guns that might be used against them in the future.

The cowards who led the charge on to the boat then tried to negotiate themselves a truce by offering up what the UDA were after. Cash and guns were offered as a bargaining tool. It sickened me.

I wasn't having bad days, I was having bad hours. It just kept coming and coming. The betrayal from closest friends followed by the eviction of the family hit me like hammer blows. If the UDA had got their hands on a main player in C Company and executed them, I doubt they would have forced the rest of them off the Shankill. But it was too late now.

The cops stopped Gina's car and searched it the moment it rolled off the pier and into Scotland. They seized £70,000 under the Proceeds of Crime Act, deeming the cash to belong to her, not any of the other four people in the car.

After a couple of days in Scotland, the convoy of cars left for England and ended up in Bolton. Once they had left the Shankill, there was no going back. They might have thought they could negotiate their way back to Belfast but the UDA were just going to take them for everything they had and finish off C Company for good.

Every day my cell door would open at 8am and I had to find something to occupy my mind and take away the pain of what had happened. I couldn't come out of my cell and talk things through with another prisoner. I was on my own.

Every day I would go to the exercise yard and run to try to put it all to the back of my mind. If I was physically fit, I thought, I might be able to cope with it mentally. Routine was the key. The wing was spotless because I mopped and cleaned it every day. Letters flooded in from supporters and I made sure I replied to everyone. I had practically no visitors because the UDA threatened to kill anyone who came to see me in prison.

For weeks, there was nothing but speculation in the papers and on the television about why my family had been forced out of the Shankill and what was going to happen next. To get my head round what was going on, I tried to speak to Gina every day and keep up to date with what their plan was. But every door was being slammed shut and nobody wanted anything to do with them.

Prisoners were allowed to call only two telephone numbers, to prevent us from organising crime from behind bars. The governor made an allowance for me because I had no idea where I could get hold of my family. Gina had to keep changing her mobile number, so a lot of the time it was only when the screws gave me the latest number that I was able to make contact.

Although the UDA had forced everyone off the Shankill, there hadn't been any revenge for the murder of Grugg and they weren't going to let that situation continue for ever. I told Gina to warn the young lads in Bolton that they should cut all ties with the UDA and get rid of their mobile-phone sim cards. The only thing that would come of any contact was trouble. But, as the weeks went on, homesickness was setting in and calls kept being made back to Northern Ireland.

Gina was one of the first to get a house. She took the top floor while Jonathan and four or five of his pals stayed downstairs.

Back in Belfast, a plan was hatched to launch an attack on the house. A lorry driver who moved between Belfast and Blackpool was used to first bring the gun across and then transport the gunman over. The wall at the back of the house was only about four feet high and the gunman had a pop through the window, hoping to get one of the lads. Luckily, the intended targets were all in another room. The word was, the gunman was from the north Belfast UDA and used a 9mm that belonged to C Company.

The UDA issued a statement saying the attack was part of its investigations into the murder by C Company of the Loyalist brigadier John Gregg. It said, 'Last night an ASU of the UFF attempted to oust members of the Adair faction in Bolton, England. As the investigation continues and more evidence is uncovered, action will be taken against anyone providing guns or a safe haven for these outcasts. They will be moved on wherever they are.'

It was a nightmare for Gina. The shooting was all over the news and it only made the people in Bolton want her out even sooner. Scene-of-crime officers were at the house for over a week, whereas I doubt they would even have bothered showing up in Belfast. Stuck in my cell, I was racked with guilt because I wasn't there to protect them and there was nothing I could do.

Chief Superintendent Don Brown, the divisional commander in Bolton, appealed for the public not to panic. He told the press, 'We would like to reassure local residents as we believe this is an isolated incident, although extra officers will be on patrol in the area over the next few days.'

It made no difference to local opinion.

In June, the UDA got the revenge they so badly wanted. One of the first who had jumped ship when he got wind there was going to be a move on C Company worked on one of Jonathan's pals, Alan McCullough, and convinced him everything would be fine for him to return to Belfast. I only knew Alan through my son. For a time, he and his girlfriend stayed with Gina. In the end, the house became too cramped and, when none of the others who had been evicted would put him up, the couple moved to Blackpool.

The longer they were away from home, the worse the pressure got. The cops were all over them, accommodation was tough to come by and money even harder. Alan figured he was only 21 and the UDA would only be interested in going after the main men in C Company to avenge Grugg. In his naivety, he believed the word coming from Belfast.

The key to luring him back was convincing there was a

tout who, far from being in exile, was in regular contact with the UDA back home and was selling the rest of them down the river to save his own back.

Even though Alan was homesick, there still had to be something major to convince him it was safe to go back to Belfast. When he touched down at the airport and walked through to Arrivals, the first thing the man who met him did was hand him a mobile phone with the tout on the other end. Alan only held the phone for a split second but it was long enough to prove the tout had been in touch with them all along. He had been let in on what was really going on and now he felt he was safe.

For a few weeks, everything was looking good for Alan. They bought him a car and told him to keep his head down for a bit, which he did, staying with his mother. She warned him that the man who had met him at the airport was trouble and shouldn't be trusted but he ignored her. After blending back in for a while, he thought everything would be fine.

Alan's body was found in a shallow grave in the Mallusk area of Belfast. Hours before he was killed, he left the house with two senior UDA figures. They later told police they had taken him for a drink and something to eat and after they parted company they hadn't seen him again. His body was discovered under inches of earth on barren land. Not long afterwards, the UFF called a newsroom in the city and admitted the murder. Alan was taken to a spot where the UDA thought C Company weapons had been stashed, and he had posed for the UFF calendar.

Alan was only a kid and it was uncalled for. He was murdered out of frustration that there had been no revenge for Grugg. It was also a message to the rest of the exiles that there was no going back. But the UDA wouldn't let it lie there. On the day of Alan's funeral, they sent death threats to the family, including his girlfriend, Suzanne, who cuddled their two-year-old daughter as his coffin was carried from his mother's house. The UDA warned there was going to be more bloodshed because the McCullough family had co-operated with the police investigation. Cops stood guard at both ends of their street and quickly dealt with a bomb hoax designed to disrupt the funeral. The UDA's behaviour was sickening.

Little Alan was three months old when his father was murdered by the INLA as he left his house to take his daughter to school. The McCullough family had sacrificed so much for the Loyalist cause. Alan's brother Kenny told the press, 'The police gave me information about my own protection and security and said they would intensify their security presence in the area. They just have no respect for anybody at all. My mother went through this 22 years ago with my father and they are just showing a complete disregard for my mother and what she went through.'

When things quietened down, Gina tried to visit me regularly in Maghaberry. The UDA were terrified I was plotting from my cell and again issued their threat to kill anyone who came to see me. After one of her visits, I turned on the television to see the police smashing their way into the house in Bolton. Drugs squad officers had waited for Gina to leave the mainland and decided to batter their way through the front door in the full glare of the news cameras. Jonathan and his pals had been snared dealing drugs, but because they were all under Gina's roof she was implicated in the pushing. I had no idea Jonathan was dealing drugs, but, if I had, a stop would have been put to it straight away. The police went through a number of addresses but predictably ours was the only one the reporters turned up at. A PR stunt for the cops, who wanted us anywhere but on their patch.

I called Gina at once and told her to go to the police station, give them fingerprints and tell them it was nothing to do with her. The detectives would be desperate to implicate her and get the kids taken into care. Scales had been taken from the house and if they found her dabs on them there would be big trouble.

I spoke on the phone to Chloe, who was panicking that she was going to be abandoned. I promised her everything would be fine, but I knew there was no guarantee it would be. I'd reached a new level of helplessness. I was well used to the four walls of a prison cell but now they were closing in on me.

Gina reported to the police station and gave them her side of the story. The investigating officers ignored the fact there were kids involved, charged her and locked her up overnight. When I heard the news I really feared the worst. It was a long night before I got the news back that she had been granted bail and while she was away from home a neighbour had been kind enough to look after the kids.

In March 2004, Jonathan admitted selling heroin and crack cocaine to undercover police officers who visited him dressed as junkies on four occasions over a two-month period. He had looked at it as a chance to make a quick buck and I doubt he had any idea of the seriousness of what he was doing. In the house, the cops found a crossbow and body armour, which belonged to me, making the case against him look even stronger.

Judge Brian Carter QC sentenced Jonathan to five years at a young offenders' institution. Before having him taken down, he said, 'The relatively small amounts of drugs indicate that this isn't anywhere near the top of a large, sophisticated drugs operation. Having said that, the wrong message must not go out. I seek to emphasise that my public duty requires me to pass a deterrent sentence to try and reduce this kind of criminality.'

Benjamin Dowie got five years while William Truesdale got four. The cops were delighted with the length of the sentences. Outside the court, Chief Superintendent Dave Lea said, beaming, 'These men were determined to try and flood Bolton with Class A drugs and the sentences show that we won't tolerate this type of criminal activity in our town. The residents of Bolton have the right to live without fear of criminals operating in their area.'

What the boys got was way over the top and in October Jonathan had his term reduced by 15 months. Nevertheless, he was 19 years old and locked up in a prison where he knew nobody. I wrote to him as often as I could to try to keep his spirits up and every Monday I got a chance to speak to him on the phone. He knew he had done wrong and took the sentence on the chin.

The hardest blow of the lot came when Gina was told she had ovarian cancer. She had nobody to give her support apart from the kids and the guilt ate away at me. I pleaded with the prison authorities to fly me over to England just for the day so I could see her but they refused. All I wanted was three hours, handcuffed at all times, but no matter what I said it wasn't going to happen. I needed to be there to help and support her and my request was refused point-blank.

Gina didn't let it get her down and was incredibly brave through it all. Every morning the kids were packed off to school and then she would get the bus to Manchester for treatment. She handled it in a matter-of-fact way. There was a problem and it had to be dealt with. I just wish I'd been there. The prison bosses were worried about my mental state and sent in a psychiatrist to assess how I was doing. He offered me medication to deal with the stress that had been building. My first reaction was to refuse it but when he pestered me I relented and took the pill from him. They also put me on suicide watch, not because I was depressed but because they thought I had to crack under the pressure at some point. In the morning when the guard unlocked my cell, I handed him back the pill. If I hadn't been 100 per cent strong, I would have gone under.

My release after two years in isolation couldn't have come soon enough. The cops were terrified about what I was going to do when I was freed and came to see what I was planning. I didn't really know. They weren't convinced and warned me that the minute I walked out people were going to be trying to kill me. What was new about that? The security services wanted me to leave and never come back. In the end, they took me themselves.

Two days before my release my cell door opened at 6am. I was half awake and had no idea at all what was going on. After searching me, they ordered me to put my clothes on. They took me out of my cell and put me into another one. I was handed a brand-new bulletproof jacket and told to put it on. I looked at the guard and asked if they were requesting me to put it on or telling me.

One of the guards, who was well over six foot, stepped forward and peeled back his outer jacket to reveal a Kevlar vest underneath. 'You're going, so get it on and let's move,' he said.

The security services were certain the threats on my life were genuine, so they decided to move me early, before those who wanted me dead knew what was going on.

As well as the vest I was given a jacket with a hood and was told just before I stood outside the wing that I was to pull it up over my head. All my belongings were stuffed into a grip they provided, then I was handcuffed and walked to the door.

Outside were blacked-out police cars waiting to take me to the RAF base at Aldergrove. The journey was only a short one along country roads but they were taking no chances. As we negotiated our way along the tight bends, a team of SAS soldiers shadowed us, watching for anyone who wasn't supposed to be there. The copper who was running the show insisted that when I got out of the car I was to put another jacket over my head again, to make sure nobody spotted me and that I wasn't seeing anything I shouldn't in the airbase.

I was taken to a cell where they took the body armour and the oversized coat off me. I was to be transported out of Northern Ireland in a military helicopter and dumped in England, where they hoped I would stay. I was taken through a safety debriefing and told to put on the army-issue grey boiler suit, helmet and life jacket. Right up until the last minute, the security services were still asking me what my plan was but I had nothing to say to them.

The journey to Manchester was strange. On the one hand, I was delighted to be released after two years in isolation. I'd made it through and I didn't want to be there one moment longer than I had to. The flipside was that I was effectively going into exile from my homeland. As we made our way towards England, I was saddened that it had come to this. I'd dedicated my life to the Loyalist cause and fighting the Republicans. I would have happily died for many of the people I had fought alongside. But all that was gone now. Lifelong pals had stabbed me in the back and I was no longer welcome in the place I'd given my all to defend.

Greater Manchester Police were waiting for me when we touched down, with blacked-out cars and a hood to conceal my identity. I was taken to Horwich, on the outskirts of Bolton, where the cops took a mugshot of me and made it plain they weren't happy about my being there. If I stepped over the line, they were going to be waiting to stamp down on me as hard as they could.

It was the first time I'd seen Gina in over a year. She hadn't long come through her operation and she had wasted away to just about nothing. I was shocked at how badly it had affected her. The weight had dropped off her, but it wasn't just the cancer. It was the pain of being forced out of her home, trying to settle where she wasn't wanted and having to do it while I was languishing behind bars. I had to hide in the house for a couple of days because the press were everywhere, trying to get pictures of me.

It didn't take long to realise I'd swapped HMP Maghaberry for HMP Bolton. It was a nightmare. I was soon getting into a routine, the same sort of routine I used to get me through a day in prison, like going to the gym. I wasn't allowed to go to the local school and pick up my kids because the parents didn't want me there. I had to sit in the car while Gina went to the gate. The police came to the house at least once a week to see what I was up to. The way I looked at it, I just wanted to keep my head down. I'd lost a bond with my kids when they were younger because I was away too often or locked up. It was different now. I wasn't wearing body armour and there were no bodyguards. It was just me, my wife and the kids, and I really wanted to make an effort with Jay, the fourth child I had with Gina.

To begin with, the cops were fine and I had no problem letting them into the house. But it wasn't long before they were giving me a hard time. We tried to rent a couple of houses but the landlord was told who we were and of course the deals fell through. The cops were listening into my phone line as well and knew I was making arrangements to make prison visits. The jails would be called and I would suddenly find out I was banned. It was becoming clear that they wanted me to become someone else's problem.

I found a surveillance camera trained on the house from a door across the road. It stood out a mile. It has been covered in fresh paint and there was a small hole that the lens peeped through. That was the last straw. I wasn't going to have the police taking the piss out of me. They were told that without a warrant they weren't getting into the house. I didn't mention the discovery of the camera and let them think they knew who was coming and going from the house.

They turned up at the door one night wearing bulletproof vests and telling me the house had to be evacuated straight away. An ASU had been sent to England and, according to their intelligence, an attempt on my life was imminent. The officer in charge instructed me to get out of the house immediately and leave the lights on to fool the gunmen into thinking I was still there. I sent them away. I had more experience of threats than they did and, more importantly, I knew what the UDA were capable of. The only way they were going to get anyone near enough to kill me was if I was betrayed by someone close to me and I was sure that hadn't happened. I would need to be offered up on a plate for them to have any chance of success.

The UDA did sent a team over to try to blow up Jackie

Thompson in his car. A train driver called Stanley Curry was given 20 years when the device he planted failed to go off and forensic teams found his DNA all over the bomb.

I'm not scared of any of them. I know better than anyone what makes them tick and they don't have what it takes. While I was inside, I vowed to confront those who had turned their backs on me. I returned to Belfast and knocked on the door of one of them early in the morning to see what he had to say for himself. The light came on inside and when he looked out and realised it was me he hid under the bed. Unless he had ten men backing him up, he was never going to say anything to me. I was there with a photographer to back me up and that was all, yet he still didn't have the nerve to come out and speak to me.

The UDA knew I was in the country that time and had scores of men scouring the streets trying to find me. I got in and out before they knew what had happened. Hours later, ten carloads of men turned up at the hotel I'd been staying at in Portadown. Like men possessed, they demanded to know where I was. Now, with a bit of back-up, they had rediscovered their bottle, but I was long gone.

Eventually, the Bolton exiles turned their backs on me as well. Sham Millar knew the day would come when I was released and he would have to explain why he tried to cut a deal with the UDA. He couldn't face me and got someone to contact the police and tell them I was threatening them. I was on remand for 39 days before admitting harassment of Kerry Thompson and Stephen McQuaid. The pair of them claimed they felt their lives were in danger.

The prosecutor told the court, 'Here we have a group of people who, because of the Troubles in Northern Ireland, have been forced to make a new life on the mainland. Some have made their home in Bolton, including the defendants. Those people fall into two camps. Those who have seized the opportunity to start a new life and those who are trying to keep the ethos that the others left behind in Belfast. This has led to the harassment of those trying to distance themselves from their former lifestyles.'

Sham got what he wanted and I was ordered to stay away from them. But the ultimate betrayal was still to come.

17

THE PEACE DIVIDEND

Gina and I were together for 24 years and we have four kids. A lot of that time I was locked up, which made our relationship very hard. It's no secret that we were unfaithful to each other on numerous occasions in equal measure. But despite that we still loved each other very much and without her support I wouldn't have made it through some very dark times. Special Branch knew the nature of our relationship and did what they could to use it to their advantage.

Back in 1990, Gina had been taken to Castlereagh at the same time that I was pulled in for questioning in connection with the murder of John Judge. The UDA shot him dead at the gate of his house as he shielded his two sons. It was claimed at the time that he was a known IRA bomber but this was denied by his family. The gunmen used Lanark

Way, as did many ASUs from both sides, to get in and out of the Falls. Eventually, after a lengthy campaign, security gates were put in place and closed between 5pm and 8am to stop it being used at night.

The female detective who interrogated Gina came into the interview room where I was being held and lost the plot. Her face was red and her eyes fixed on me as she screamed at me, 'You're going to get her killed. I don't care about you but what is going to happen to her when the IRA come to get you? They will take one look through the obscured glass in the window and open fire. They won't stop to think is it you or her. You're the same height, so they'll just open up. How are you going to live with that?'

The copper had to be pulled out of the room because she was taking it very personally. I could see the hatred in her eyes. She would have killed me there and then if she'd thought she could get away with it.

The detectives claimed Gina had admitted possessing guns and allowing our house to be used by the UFF. If I admitted some sort of role in the Judge murder, they would let her walk. That was the game they wanted to play. I knew Gina wouldn't have admitted anything, so I suggested if they had enough on her they should charge her. This got under their skin no end. The detectives knew I was playing them at their own game, being a smart-arse, and there was nothing they could do about it.

But I wasn't using her. Gina and I both accepted that we didn't live in a suburban street and have dinner parties at the weekend. She knew I was married not just to her but to the UDA as well, and she accepted everything that went along with it. It drove the security people mad.

When I was held for directing terrorism, Special Branch knew they had me in a tight spot and as an extra 'up yours' they told Gina I was having an affair. It was our first major bust-up and I bet the cops loved it. Then came the time when they asked Gina if she knew a woman called Jackie 'Legs' Robinson from Taughmonagh. They already knew the answer and so did Gina. She wasn't going to give them the satisfaction of knowing they had got to her but it had.

I'd been seeing Jackie and she had fallen for me in a big way; so much so that she later claimed we were an item for nine years. I enjoyed the attention she gave me and that was about it. Before I was locked up, I saw her at the most every ten days but she became obsessed with me. Jackie visited me at the Maze all the time, trying to move in on my life. She went as far as getting an engagement ring and telling everyone we were going to get hitched. Over and over, she insisted that we were going to live happily ever after and she was going to have my child. I was just starting a 16-year sentence. The prospects weren't great.

It wasn't until I was locked up that I realised how much Gina meant to me. I knew I loved her and the kids, but now they were out of reach it dawned on me just how much. I thought I was mentally strong and would be able to cope. When Gina said she was leaving me, I told her I didn't care, but for 18 months it ate away at me. I was locked up and there was nothing I could do about it. She was seeing other people and I was lying in the Maze wondering what she was up to at night and who she was with. I was humiliated but I could do nothing. I don't think I ever got over it. Even when we got married, it was at the back of my mind, nagging away at me.

In February 1997, we got hitched. Gina had claimed she had made a mistake and that really she wanted to be my wife. We had the kids together and nobody could ever take that away from us. That was true. They were the most important thing to me. But the wedding would prove to be a mistake. At the time, I was happy and we promised there would be no more cheating and we would try to make a proper go of it.

Our wedding day was special. Gina arrived at the Maze in a stretch limo and was brought up to the prison church for the ceremony. It was as close to a proper wedding as you could get while being inside. Sam McCrory was my best man and we both hired top hat and tails to look the part. The two of us stood at the altar as Gina entered in a full wedding dress and was walked up the aisle by her brother. The kids were all dressed up and there were flowers everywhere. The prison wardens gave us plenty of space and let us bring in as much booze as we wanted. The kitchen staff made us a cake and there was a ghetto-blaster to play Gina's favourite UB40 song, 'I Got You Babe', for the first dance.

For three hours, we were surrounded by our friends and family and were almost able to forget where we were. Afterwards, Gina went back to our house on the Shankill and had a party with her pals while we returned to the wing and continued the celebrations.

THE PEACE DIVIDEND

For a while, everything was fine between us. We had Jay and played at happy families. It was still tough being locked up and not seeing each other. It wasn't a normal relationship but we did our best to make it work. Under the Good Friday Agreement, I was allowed out and it eased the pressure. It was only when I was returned to Maghaberry the second time that the cracks began to show.

By then, Gina and the rest of the family had been evicted and had settled in Bolton. A lad called Wayne Dowie and one of his brothers, both of whom had been chased off the Shankill, were under the same roof for a while and it was then that Gina started seeing Dowie. It all came out one night when I was talking to her on the phone and she let slip that they had all been on a night out and she had got a taxi back on her own with him. I'm not sure what it was but I knew something was wrong. I didn't need it pointed out to me: I just knew.

I argued with her on the phone and told her I thought she was cheating on me. But she convinced me I was paranoid and being locked up in isolation was messing with my head. I had plenty of time to think in the cell on my own and eventually gave her the benefit of the doubt and came to the conclusion I was over-reacting. I didn't really know Dowie that well. When he was charged with the murder of Jonathan Stewart during the second Loyalist feud and was remanded in Maghaberry, I put what had happened behind me. His family life was a mess and hardly anyone came to visit him, so I wrote to him and stuck some money on to his allowance to try to keep his spirits up.

I was released before Dowie and, when he first got out, he went to Scotland and we paid for him to fly down to stay with us. He had nowhere else to go. I didn't have a problem with it. My life was all over the place after all the treachery I'd been through with C Company, but the one person I thought I could trust was Gina. I didn't see any reason to worry.

Dowie's mother also came over from Belfast to see him. I stood at Liverpool Airport with a bottle of champagne to welcome him back and there was a big party waiting for him at the house. Dowie arrived with nothing, so I gave him some of my clothes and when I had a few quid spare I took him to the shops to buy his own. Dowie and Jonathan became best mates and the two of them would go to the gym and train together. The last thing I thought was that he was messing about with my wife.

It came to a head when I was given 39 days for harassment. Sitting in my cell, I started running over all the little things again. The way they behaved with each other and seemed to have their own private jokes. Over and over, I thought about it. I was sure something was going on.

Gina still denied it and told me I was losing my mind. Everything that had happened to me was now taking its toll, she said, and I was losing my grip on reality. She told me the betrayals had pushed me to the edge and now all I could see around me were traitors and liars, when the people who were left were the most loyal.

For six weeks, I thought about nothing else in my cell. Dowie even came on the phone and insisted there was nothing going on. Gina called Skelly and told him I was losing the plot as well.

When I finished the sentence, I wanted to go home and get it all sorted out, but Gina insisted we go to the pub and celebrate. It was going fine; Sam and a few other pals showed up and the booze was flowing. As I got drunker, Gina became braver and started taunting me about Dowie, cuddling up to him and saying she loved him as a friend. But then she let slip something that confirmed they had been seeing each other. The next thing all hell broke loose and she and I were getting stuck into each other.

She started punching me first but I didn't hold back. It wasn't long until the cops turned up and I was taken to the police station. I was back in a cell wondering if my head really had gone. I couldn't really remember what state I left Gina in. My face had cuts all over it. I was disgusted and humiliated about what I'd done. The fact I'd sunk so low and hit a woman seemed to confirm I was losing the plot.

Before the fight, Sam told me I needed to sort myself out and Gina would never do anything like that to me, because we had been through too much together. When he saw what happened, he went back to Scotland, furious that he had made the effort to make sure I had a good party to celebrate my release and ended up fighting with Gina. He wanted nothing to do with me. I was convinced the cops were going to lock me up until a trial and that I was facing six months.

During the interview, the investigating officers said I'd pulled out some of Gina's hair during the brawl and they showed me a picture of her. There wasn't a mark on her, but the fact that she had escaped a bruise or a cut didn't excuse what I'd done. I don't pretend I feel anything other than shame about what happened. Drunk or not, my behaviour was unacceptable. But the police knew it was more complicated than domestic violence and I was bailed. The moment I got out, I went home to have it out with Gina.

Nobody knew why I'd lost the plot or even that I thought she was messing about with Dowie. They were convinced I was losing it and was lashing out for no reason at all. I phoned Sam to try to clear the air and I found myself agreeing with everything he said, that I needed to sort my head out before I made more mistakes. I accepted there was nothing going on. I had to speak to Dowie, though, to put my mind at ease.

The following day, the two of us went for a walk round a local park and talked. He promised there was nothing going on and said he was embarrassed about the whole situation. Now I'd spoken to the two of them, I came to the decision to let it go and accepted that it had been my fault. I went back to the house and apologised to Gina and said she was right, things had been getting on top of me and in the end it had become too much for me to take. I was going to do my best to make sure I kept a grip of things and there would be no more incidents.

Gina was happy at that and I went downstairs. Jonathan, Dowie and I had a few beers before I decided to go to bed. When I got into the room, she was already asleep but her mobile was beeping. I went over to have a look and there was a text from Dowie: 'Gina please don't let him near you tonight. It will kill me if you do. Wayne.' I felt the blood drain from my face. Everything I thought was going on was. I was right. The thing that hurt the most was that they had tried to convince me I was losing the plot and, not only that, they had tried to turn my best mate against me.

I went downstairs and asked Dowie if I could have a word with him. I took him into the bathroom for a bit of privacy. He thought everything was fine. Then I showed him the phone. Speechless, he turned his head away. I was within an inch of my doing something I would regret for the rest of my life. Something told me to back off. If something had happened to Dowie, there was no way I was going to get away with it. The cops were red hot on me already and there was a camera trained on the door. There was only one person who was going to get the blame.

I woke Gina. She didn't know what was going on but played it cool anyway. I showed her the phone. Dowie was in the room looking agitated, waiting to see what was going to happen next. I put everything to Gina. She had been cheating on me, denied it and told me I was losing it to protect her sordid little affair. After a moment of weighing up the options, she admitted to the lot and said she didn't want to be with me any more.

I was relieved I wasn't losing my mind but it soon hit me: our relationship was over. I couldn't force her to love me. Dowie still hadn't uttered a word. I imagine it was the last place on the planet he wanted to be: in my bedroom as my wife was telling me she loved him instead. I think if she had told me it was over I probably wouldn't have had a problem with that. It was the fact that she twisted everything against me. I could have kicked holes out of either of them but I didn't. Dowie legged it the first chance he got. Later, I phoned him and told him he could come and pick his stuff up. He thought it was a trap and didn't show.

For two days, I tried to find it in me to stay and forgive her but I couldn't. Every time I looked at her, all I saw was the misery she had put me through. I got in the car with two grip bags and drove to Scotland. When Jonathan found out what had happened, he followed me up to Scotland.

A couple of months later, the court case came up. Bolton Magistrates' Court was told that I'd 'removed a fairly large quantity of hair from her head' by dragging Gina across the floor of the pub. She admitted to officers that I had attacked her but said she didn't want to make a complaint. But they were able to prosecute me on the strength of witness statements. The court was also told that I was 'deeply sorry and ashamed' of what had happened and I had 'never been convicted of any domestic violence or any offences against his family. He accepted that after the initial self-defence he over-reacted'.

Now I'm settled in Scotland, I don't feel I have to run and hide from anyone. I live here openly and have no fears of attempts on my life. The police have warned me once since I have been in Ayrshire, but it came to nothing. The war is over for the IRA, and the UDA has become fractured and ineffective. I'm currently living under a Loyalist death sentence but I don't give it a second thought and sleep soundly at night. The last time they sent someone over to have a dash at me and the people around me, the bomb he planted failed to go off and he is now doing 20 years in prison. The next man who comes to fire a shot or leave a device is going to have to think about the consequences.

Out of Belfast, I'm able to get on with my life, something I've never been able to do in the past. There is no more looking over my shoulder waiting for the next attack or listening for the rumble of the police armoured vehicles coming to lift me before dawn. I'm a big boy now and if I break the law and get caught I know I'll go to jail.

The only regret I have is putting my life on the line and spending so many years behind bars for people who turned their backs on me. It would be false of me to say I regret being a paramilitary and being involved. I don't. When the Combined Loyalist Military Command offered 'abject and true' remorse to victims of violence during the Troubles, I agreed and still do. I genuinely want Northern Ireland to have peace and I urge all young people not to take up a life of violence, but to work to keep the peace. I know one day I'll be back to enjoy it. I have no role to play in the community any more and nor do I want to. My actions and those of C Company forced the IRA to come to the table and talk.

I have always said the problems and the people who opposed me and threw me out of my home will go away. One by one, they have fallen. Gregg and Gray are dead. William 'Mo' Courtney was taken to court for the murder of McCullough but the case was thrown out and an appeal by the prosecution and at the time of writing was still ongoing. Without my putting my finger on a trigger, they are taking care of my problems by themselves.

Make no mistake: I will be back.

KEY CHARACTERS

Adair (nee Crossan), Gina: former wife of Johnny and mother of four children by him: Jonathan, Natalie, Jay and Chloe.

Adams, Gerry: President of Sinn Fein and abstentionist MP for West Belfast at Westminster.

Adgey, Derek: one-time Royal Marine.

Bcggs, Tommy 'Shirt and Tie Man': tailor (by day) and driver for C Company, UDA.

Bratty, Joe: senior member of south Belfast UDA.

Brown, Detective Sergeant Jonty: officer of RUC's north Belfast murder squad, who claimed personal responsibility for bringing Adair to justice for 'directing terrorism'.

Copeland, Eddie: Republican activist in north Belfast.

Dodds, William 'Winkie': commander of C Company, UDA.

Dromgoole, Maurice: friend of Adair, killed in car accident in 1985.

Drumgoole, Gerry: member of C Company, UDA.

Finucane, Pat: Republican lawyer and alleged IRA member murdered in Belfast in 1989.

Flanagan, Sir Robbie: Chief Constable of RUC

Mac: senior member of C Company, UDA, and agent of Special Branch.

Gallagher, Gino: leader of INLA.

Gillen, Brian: leading Republican militant in Northern Ireland.

Gray, Jim: commander of east Belfast UDA.

Gregg, John 'Grugg': brigadier of south-east Antrim UDA and member of UDA Inner Council, murdered in 2003.

Hodgen, Donald: head of security of C Company, UDA.

Kerr, Alec: member of UDA Inner Council.

Mandelson, Peter: successor to Dr Marjorie Mowlam as Secretary of State for Northern Ireland.

Martindale, Detective Superintendent Derek: head of CID.

Maskey, Alex: Sinn Fein councillor.

McCrory, Sam 'Skelly': member of C Company, UDA.

McGuinness, Martin: deputy leader of Sinn Fein and former Minister of Education in Northern Ireland Executive.

McMaster, Gary: senior member of C Company, UDA.

McMichael, John: second in command of UDA, killed by IRA bomb in 1987.

Millar, James 'Sham': member of C Company, UDA.

Mowlam, Dr Marjorie 'Mo': Secretary of State for Northern Ireland.

Murphy, Paul: successor to Dr John Reid as Secretary of State for Northern Ireland.

Nelson, Brian: chief intelligence officer of UDA and agent of FRU; previously British Army soldier.

O'Prey, Martin 'Rook': member of IPLO, murdered in 1991.

Payne, Davey: former UDA man and a key member of Crumlin Road Opportunities youth work scheme; sentenced in 1988 to 19 years in prison for arms smuggling.

Reid, Dr John: successor to Peter Mandelson as Secretary of State for Northern Ireland.

Robinson, Jackie 'Legs': lover of Adair.

Rosborough, Mark: friend of Adair, murdered in 1985.

Smallwoods, Ray: chairman of Ulster Democratic Party.

McKeag, Steve 'Top Gun': senior member of C Company, UDA.

Spruce, Katherine: lover of Adair who provided RUC with information on him which failed to secure his conviction.

Stakeknife: codename of leading Republican agent.

Stevens, John: Deputy Chief Constable of Cambridgeshire Police and author of three reports, including one on links between UK security forces in Northern Ireland and UDA in killing of Pat Finucane.

Stobie, Billy: quartermaster of UDA.

Stone, Michael: Loyalist terrorist sentenced to 638 years in prison for murdering three people at Milltown Cemetery in Belfast in 1988, and released under the Good Friday Agreement in July 2000. At the time of writing, in jail for attempted murder after illegally entering the parliament building at Stormont while armed in November 2006.

Thompson, Jackie: member of C Company, UDA, and self-appointed successor to Adair as brigadier of west Belfast UDA.

Tyrie, Andy: Supreme Commander and Chairman of UDA from 1973 to 1988.

Wright, Billy: leader of mid-Ulster UVF and later of LVF, murdered in Maze Prison in 1997.

GLOSSARY

12 July: commonly accepted as the commemoration of the Battle of the Boyne in 1690. In more general terms the decisive victory in 1691 of Protestant King William III (see 'King Billy') over Catholic exciled King James II at Battle of Aughrim in County Galway, Ireland.

APC: armoured personnel carrier.

ASU: active service unit, a small team engaged in paramilitary operations.

DUP: Democratic Unionist Party, Loyalist political party in Northern Ireland.

FRU: Force Research Unit, intelligence unit of British Army.

Good Friday Agreement: historic accord between governments of UK and Ireland and political parties in Northern Ireland on governance of the province, signed on 10 April 1998 in Belfast.

INLA: Irish National Liberation Army, Republican paramilitary group.

IPLO: Irish People's Liberation Organisation, Republican paramilitary group.

IRA: Irish Republican Army, paramilitary group.

King Billy: William III, anti-Catholic King of England from 1689 to 1702 (see '12 July').

Loyalist: professing allegiance to United Kingdom and its monarchy.

LVF: Loyalist Volunteer Force, Loyalist paramilitary group.

Nationalist: proponent of a united Ireland embracing the Republic of Ireland and the six counties of Northern Ireland, or Ulster, currently part of the United Kingdom. Also called Republican.

Provos: Provisional IRA, Republican paramilitary group.

Real IRA: Republican paramilitary group.

Red Hand Commando: Loyalist paramilitary group, an offshoot of the UVF.

Red Hand Defenders: Loyalist paramilitary group which emerged after the Good Friday Agreement.

Republican: proponent of a united Ireland embracing the Republic of Ireland and the six counties of Northern Ireland, or Ulster, currently part of the United Kingdom. Also called Nationalist.

RUC: Royal Ulster Constabulary, the police force of Northern Ireland.

SDLP: Social Democratic and Labour Party, Nationalist political party in Northern Ireland.

GLOSSARY

Sinn Fein ('We Ourselves'): Republican political party in Northern Ireland.

Special Branch: arm of each police force with responsibility for national security.

UDA: Ulster Defence Association, Loyalist paramilitary group. The UFF was the military wing. Belfast was split into different brigades and then into companies.

UDF: Ulster Defence Force, Loyalist paramilitary group.

UDP: Ulster Democratic Party, Loyalist political party in Northern Ireland.

UDR: Ulster Defence Regiment, Loyalist infantry regiment of the British Army strongly identified with the Protestant and unionist community